Narrative Elements
and
Religious Meanings

Wesley A. Kort

Narrative Elements
and
Religious Meanings

Fortress Press Philadelphia

Library of Congress Catalog Card Number 75–15257

ISBN (Paper) 0-8006-1433-X

5111E75   Printed in the U.S.A.   1-1433 (Paper)

JANTINA SCHRIK KORT

Maar Jeruzalem, dat boven is, dat is vrij,

hetwelk is ons aller moeder. . . .

Contents

Preface

Enough work has now been done in religion and literature to demonstrate that talk about the power and meaning of literary texts regularly and easily involves a critic in discussions of morality and religion. And enough theologians have taken an interest in literary works and criticism to suggest that religion is attracted to literature. Most attempts to account for this mutual attraction and involvement have found their reasons in the peculiar nature of the creative act, in the role of the artist in a society. A few have found their reasons in the response of the reader to literary texts. The aim of this book is to provide an answer to the question, Why do modern narratives so often contain or imply religious or religiously suggestive meanings? That answer will arise neither from the role of the artist nor from the characteristics of literary response. It will arise, instead, from a study of the nature of narratives themselves.

Howard Harper and Robert Detweiler read an earlier version of this work, and I am very grateful to them for their suggestions and encouragement. I also want to thank the faculty of the Department of Religion at the University of Richmond for their hospitality to me and my wife during our visit there in the fall of 1972, at which time I gave as the university's annual lecture series two presentations using material found largely now in the Introduction and Conclusion to this book. I am also grateful to the Committee on International Studies at Duke University for a summer grant which allowed me to begin the work which led to this publication. Finally, I want to thank Ms. Diane Mowrey for the help she gave me in proofreading the manuscript.
Duke University
March, 1975

Introduction

Anyone interested in the possibility of bringing into focus the religious meaning or significance of a narrative is faced immediately with questions like these: Why do narratives actually or potentially have religious meaning or significance? Where is that meaning to be found and from what is the religious significance derived? When is it legitimate or even necessary to make a narrative's religious meaning or significance a part of the hermeneutical act?

What should be avoided on the way to some answers to these questions are roads that lead to theoretical dead ends. Of these, one that is commonly taken begins with or leads to a form-content split, dividing the narrative against itself, separating its literary form from its religious meaning or significance. Another and equally limiting approach is to address narratives with some religiously significant problem or idea and to measure them by it. Still another is to limit one's attention to narratives which have recognizable religious words, to limit the possibility of religious meaning or significance to a special, gathered group of literary works. A contrary, but equally unpromising way follows upon the assertion that anything aesthetic is therefore religiously important, an assertion that results in as few distinctions and as little clarity to the subject as its secular counterpart, namely, the formalist contention that religious matters in literary texts are aesthetic and no longer religiously significant at all.

The purpose of this study is to hold open an approach that will avoid these dead ends. The thesis of the study is that modern narratives can so often be found to carry or imply religious or religiously suggestive meanings because the elements of narrative, as well as elements of other literary forms, have a natural

1

relation to corresponding moments in religious life and thought. The method of study is to isolate the elements of narrative, to demonstrate the kind of religious meaning each tends naturally to draw to itself or by which each tends naturally to be complicated and enriched, particularly when that element is the dominant power and meaning source of a narrative, and to extend the discussion of that element out into its corresponding moment of religious life and thought.

This approach to the question of why narratives can have religious meaning or significance and what these meanings or significances are likely to be owes something to the work of Preston T. Roberts, Jr. on plot (I shall comment more fully on Roberts's work in chapter 3) and, even more, to Gerhardus Van Der Leeuw's study of the relation of religion to art.[1] Van Der Leeuw's principal theses are: (1) religion and art not only are inseparable in primitive expressions, but also are actually in need of one another for their fullest development; (2) the present separation of religion and art is due to their pursuit, in growing isolation from each other and even, at times, in defiance of one another, of possibilities most easily actualized by each; (3) in their present state of separation one can see those points, so to speak, where they once were joined, in much the same way that one can see on either wall of a canyon the corresponding marks which testify to the sides' original union.

What I take from Preston Roberts primarily and most generally is his insistence that what makes the religious meaning or significance of a literary text worth bothering about is the fact that it is actually or potentially meaningful religiously at the very root of its life, although for him that tends to be always its plot. What I take from Van Der Leeuw is primarily his insistence that religion and art have a natural (he would say original) relation to each other which can be neglected only to their eventual, mutual harm.

By limiting the discussion to narrative and the ways in which and the reasons why reflection on its elements leads naturally to complications and enrichments of a religious nature or significance, I do not intend to imply that no such case could be made

1. Gerhardus Van Der Leeuw, *Sacred and Profane Beauty: The Holy in Art*, trans. David E. Green (New York: Holt, Rinehart and Winston, 1963).

for poetry or for drama. But Van Der Leeuw included chapters on poetry and drama in his book, and, although more could be done, his is a major beginning. In addition, it can be argued that modern narrative is a comprehensive form which includes lyrical and dramatic aspects, so that some of the things to be said about the elements of narrative are relevant to poetry and drama as well. Further, by drawing my examples of narratives in which one of each of the elements is the dominant meaning and power source from works of fairly recent literature, I do not intend to suggest that it is only in this period that we find narratives of religious meaning or significance or that they are so in these ways only now. But I do think it is true that we live in a time when the laying out of the four corners of a fictional world is increasingly seen as problematic, so that implied authors or narrators appear to be conscious of and even worried about the status and meaning of setting, character, plot, and tone. The result is that they are liable to include reflection on the dominant element within the work. Surely they inherit this self-consciousness about the act of creating a fictional world, but because they appear on the scene rather late, they reveal the problematics a bit more clearly.

Of course, narratives by themselves constitute only one of the three moments in the aesthetic circle, moments which, although separable, are always pointing to or leading from one to another. And the important work which has been done in the area of religion and literature at the moments of author or of reader is not being set aside by this more text-oriented approach.[2] In fact, before going into a study of the elements of narrative, I want to call attention to some formal correlations between the aesthetic acts of writing and reading and corresponding moments in religious life and thought. By looking at the moment of creating and then at the moment of reading, a general, cumulative context, it is hoped, will develop in which an interest in the close affinities between the elements of narrative and their potential or real religious meanings or significance will more easily be taken as the natural sort of thing I think it is.

2. I have in mind the very influential work of Nathan A. Scott, Jr. on author, to which reference will be made in chapter 4, and the very suggestive book on reader by Sallie M. Te Selle, *Literature and Christian Life* (New Haven: Yale University Press, 1966). On the moment of reader see too, perhaps, my essay, "Recent fiction and the Christian Reader," *The Reformed Journal* 16, no. 7 (September, 1966): 17–19.

I

Observations which, I think, are mutually illuminating to the creative act and corresponding aspects of religious life and thought call attention to three points: identity, the desire for wholeness or totality, and an orientation toward the ineffable. Before clarifying possible correlations between the two domains at these three points I want to explain what I mean by terms I shall be using, terms such as "artist," "reader," "religious man," or "religious community." They are hypothetical. In the Conclusion I shall have more to say about the defining characteristics of religion. The terms "artist" and "reader" lack the kind of dogmatic status given their equivalents in Dorothy Sayers's influential study,[3] since, as her argument proceeds, it becomes clear that an artist is to be considered "heretical" if he lacks in interactions those contraries which her image of the artist contains. The terms "artist" and "reader" are intended as suggestive summaries of reflection on narratives, on how to account for them, and on the reasons why they are engaging. Hypothetical as they are, "reader" and "artist" stand willing to adjust to facts and judgments I may have neglected or mishandled, ready, even, to step aside at the advent of more convincing hypotheses.

There appear to be three worthwhile observations to make concerning the artist's sense of himself or his awareness of what is going on. The first of these observations is that he identifies himself as artist in response to a strong, basic sense of the situation prior to or apart from his creative work. Sometimes this situation is simply vacancy, the lack of what is about to be created; sometimes what is prior to or apart from creation is chaotic; sometimes it is an active threat, an enemy, an evil. Perhaps we are not so aware of this matter because in our own time we are expected to assume belief in the uniqueness and consequent value of every individual and his experiences and feelings, so that it goes without saying that the artist feels vacancy and threat in the situation prior to his act if only because of the simple fact that he has not yet created. It is almost inconceivable that a person so inclined or gifted would refrain from creating because he could not add anything to an already full,

3. Dorothy L. Sayers, *The Mind of the Maker* (London: Methuen and Co., 1942).

coherent, and life-enhancing world. But we cannot be so doc-
trinaire about the principle of inherent individual value to
ground the creative act, as Susanne Langer does,[4] in the desire
to express human feeling, for the act is also dependent on the
deep awareness that this new form will provide something new
or needed. Simply because we take that for granted need not
blind us to its status as a claim. The creative act is a judgment
on the state of affairs prior to the act. Similarly, there is for a
religious person or community a strong sense of what charac-
terized the situation prior to or apart from its creation, and it is
out of this sense that the distinction between sacred and secular
arises.[5] A religious community retains and rehearses its characteristic words and acts to maintain its identity against those alter-
natives of vacancy, chaos, or evil power which seem ready to
preempt their place.

A second observation worth making about identity is that
both the artist and the religious man or community feel possessed of a unique burden or capacity. This factor stands in a
dialectical relation to the sense of what lies prior to or apart
from the creative act. What is needed can be provided. The religious categories of election, mission, or destiny find correlates in
the creative act, and it is important to identify this cause for
writing, even though there may be other, though to my mind
aesthetically less interesting, reasons why writers create narratives. James Agee wrote out of a need and a capacity to see, to
listen, to speak accurately, carefully, freshly. John Updike's fiction is, among other things, an attempt to rescue moments of
value from the damnation of being forgotten. Norman Mailer is
exercised by the impersonality, dishonesty, and repetition in so
much of American life, and he exerts his considerable energy to
move language and all else that is potentially creative in human
life to the borderline of mystery.

A final observation about identity is that for both the artist
and the religious person or group the creative act actualizes
community. The discipline becomes a process in which images
of the artist and the reader are created and brought together. As

4. See Susanne K. Langer, *Problems of Art* (New York: Charles Scribner & Sons, 1957).
5. See Mircea Eliade, *The Sacred and the Profane: The Nature of Religion*, trans. Willard R. Trask (New York: Harper & Row, 1959).

Walter Ong and others have taught us,[6] the relation between artist and reader is not only of a kind based on or leading to communication, in the sense of a transfer of ideas or information or even feelings, but of a kind suggested by the word "communion." Moving out from the images of artist and reader built into a narrative, that communion can be, also, between the artist himself and his imagined reader, even if he is that reader; between the reader and the image of the artist; and even, although this leads to strange talk since rarely would the two be conscious of it, between the author and the reader. Salinger's Holden Caulfield is talking about this kind of experience when he speaks of books which, when you read them, you wish the author were some terrific friend of yours so you could call him up whenever you wanted.[7] Similarly, religious people do or should use and receive religious language and rituals not primarily for their capacity to communicate information or even ideas or feelings but to actualize wholeness, community. The actual experience of this unity, both aesthetically and religiously, is very difficult to account for, to predict, or to coerce. The creative act involves working at that rapport until it seems to happen, until the images of artist and reader meet.

This discussion of the artist's and religious man's similar interests in the culminating experience of communion leads to the second general area in which correlations between the two can be found: their interest in and conscious construction of images of wholeness, totality, and cosmos. The observations that I would like to make on this point will treat the similarities in the means used by each to actualize this interest. The first of these means is the ordering of time.

Frank Kermode, whose important book, *The Sense of an Ending,* we shall have occasion to discuss more fully in chapter 3, contends that the basic reason for the writing and the reading of fiction is to create the illusion of ordered time, of time as a whole, with a beginning and, even more importantly, with

6. See Walter J. Ong, S. J., *The Barbarian Within and Other Fugitive Essays and Studies* (New York: Macmillan Company, 1962), particularly chapter 4; and Walter Slatoff. *With Respect to Readers: Dimensions of Literary Response* (Ithaca, N.Y.: Cornell University Press, 1970).

7. Cited by Wayne C. Booth, *The Rhetoric of Fiction* (Chicago: University of Chicago Press, 1961), p. 213.

an ending.[8] He differs from the Aristotelian construing of time in fiction by his philosophical assertion about the actually unordered, even chaotic, nature of time as it is experienced. The concord which a fiction is has its origin solely in the form-making imagination acting upon disorganized time. This need to make a "whole" of time, to relate events to one another and primarily to an ending, is what accounts both for religious myth and modern fiction in Kermode's view. Any intellect or imagination which views as coincident the experience of time and its meaning or order is laboring with mythic proclivities, proclivities Kermode considers not so much anachronistic as mistaken, and even dangerous. Kermode's book brings into sharp focus the relation of fiction to religious myth on this point of making time a whole, although in another context I shall want to dispute the philosophical basis for his rejection of inherently meaningful time. It should be said, too, that artists and religious people need not be considered so resistive to chaos as Kermode makes them out to be. Religious rituals can in some of their aspects be seen, also, as a means of breaking time up, producing chaos, perhaps at the end of a year, so that the new order can be ushered in. Correspondingly, it may be the intention of a specific literary text as much to attack the inherited wholes a reader can be thought to entertain as to provide a concord. But it is also true that this disassembling work of a religious or aesthetic form is done within a specific time, and formed time, willy-nilly, has a concord-producing effect. The simple act of staking out a piece of time makes of that time something special.

A second way in which artists and religious people or communities can create wholeness and a sense of totality is through metaphor. Although metaphor is a category familiar to literary critics and theorists, particularly to those oriented to lyric poetry, it is inadequately appreciated by theorists of religion, and it may be possible to suspect that what are taken in religious life and thought to be symbols may occasionally really be metaphors. But in order for this awareness among religious theorists to occur, metaphor must be freed from the imposed limits of I. A. Richards's definition. While by no means wishing to denigrate

8. Frank Kermode, *The Sense of an Ending: Studies in the Theory of Fiction* (New York: Oxford University Press, 1967), pp. 45, 136.

the considerable work done by Richards to rescue metaphor from the slight role of providing linguistic decoration and to defend metaphor from attacks on the validity of poetic language, I think that an important aspect of metaphor is neglected by him. By relating the interaction of tenor and vehicle to the process of unifying, which is for him the first of the mental functions, he neglects an aspect or consequence of metaphor of which Alain Robbe-Grillet[9] is aware, if only in order to avoid it —namely, to create depth. The reason why disparate things are brought together in a metaphor may be not only that there is perceived to be "some direct resemblance between the two things, the tenor and vehicle," nor even because of "some common attitude which we may (often through accidental and extraneous reasons) take up towards them both,"[10] but rather it may be due to the fact that some witness is being made through this act to a hidden, unifying ground by which things separate in our experience of them are mutually rooted and sustained. The two identifiable factors of a metaphor are not necessarily held together only by their resemblances or by the force of the ordering mind; they may also be held together by a missing middle factor, the invisible bed on which the two strangers mate. It may even be the principal intention or effect of the use of metaphor to create a sense of that middle, missing factor. Metaphorical language can be unifying, then, also because it can suggest the presence of a hidden, unifying ground.

If this dimension of metaphor is understood, its role in religious life and thought can be recognized. The role of metaphor in the Old Testament Book of Proverbs, for example, may easily be to testify to an underlying unity in created life. And Jesus as Christ, who is for the Christian church at the same time both man and God, is a metaphor, a moment or figure in which two unlike things, God and man, are held together, joined by a missing middle factor which provides the church a source for endless contemplation.

9. See Alain Robbe-Grillet, *Snapshots and Towards a New Novel*, trans. Barbara Wright (London: Calder and Boyars, 1965).
10. Ivor Armstrong Richards, *The Philosophy of Rhetoric* (New York: Oxford University Press, 1936), p. 118. On the use of metaphor, see also, idem, *Principles of Literary Criticism* (London: Harcourt, Brace & Co., 1924), pp. 239–41.

Symbol, the third means by which unity and totality are achieved in both the artist's and the religious man's articulated worlds, is structurally quite different from metaphor. In a symbol that which unifies is apparent; that which is being unified is not so apparent. Potent symbols gather meaning and force by unifying contraries—light and dark, life and death, male and female, beginning and ending, good and evil. The more unifying, the more powerful a symbol is or must be. The category of image is broader than symbol; not all images are symbols.[11] Epiphany is a more particular, limited term, one clarified by Joyce and tied by Brooks and Wimsatt to Joyce's roots in Aquinas.[12] The emphasis here lies on an experience of unity and depth through total attention to the singularity, the quiddity of an individual object or event. The occasion for the epiphany lacks the public status of a symbol, and the focus of the term is on the beholder's capacity for concentration.

That image, symbol, and epiphany are important religious terms need not be labored. They are terms which, along with the ordering of time and the use of metaphors, account for the ways in which religious people satisfy, or have satisfied for them, their need and desire for wholeness and totality.

A final area in which correlations between the artist and religious people or communities can be found is in the orientation of the language in each toward the inexpressible, toward silence.

Although I shall have more to say about literary language in my discussion of tone, it should be noted here that the language of a fiction stands somewhere between what needs naming and perfect language. Below it, so to speak, is the feeling, the relationship, the scene, the possibility, whatever it is that needs to be named. Language is called forth by namelessness; something must be said. But language is also intimidated by this silence, since language will not fully actualize that potential. Above language stands the image of the perfect speaker of the perfect word—the image of Milton in Wordsworth's sonnet, *London, 1802*, for example. The silence of that image excites language into being because of the possibility of saying the right thing, of

---

11. This despite Langer's assertion in *Problems of Art*, p. 131.
12. William Wimsatt, Jr. and Cleanth Brooks, *Literary Criticism: A Short History* (New York: Alfred A. Knopf, 1957), pp. 133–34.

actualizing possibility with the perfect name. But the image of
the perfect speaker of the perfect word also intimidates language,
reflects its inadequacy. The language of a narrative, then, is in
tension with at least one, and perhaps both, of these silences—
the silence of the nursing mother whales in the deep revealed to
Ishmael and the silence of perfect form, Beatrice or Wisdom.[13]

Ihab Hassan speaks of the relation of literary language to
silence in different terms.[14] His is a kind of hot-cold distinction,
and he contends that the direction of language in a particular
work is toward one or the other of these kinds of silence, either
through expansion and extension to explosion and silence or
through reduction and limitation to contraction and silence. His
example of the first is Henry Miller and of the second is Samuel
Beckett.

The role of silence in religious language is a direct correlate
of these tensions and orientations. The religious community or
person, if and when they speak of the objects of religious experience or of that experience itself, must always be dealing with
matters beyond the reach of language, matters which both invite
naming but elude it as well. Such speaking goes on in the presence of authoritatively, and perhaps even perfectly, articulated
expressions which come down as sayings of wise and holy men
or as creeds or scriptures. And the distinction Hassan makes of
literary languages can also be made of religious uses of language.
One direction of such language is from theology to prophecy, to
saying something about everything or everything about something, to the explosion of glossolalia and then to silence; the
other direction is toward the discipline of saying more and more
with fewer and fewer words—the whole law while standing on
one foot, the Torah and Prophets in two sentences, the whole
of the tradition in one word—to the total contraction of silence.

An emphasis on the importance of silence for literary language dilutes the literary problem of the openness of a literary
form. Although the formalist insistence on the closed nature of
a work is an important one because it keeps the work from being
subservient to something else—the world outside it, the author's

13. See Wesley Kort, "The Silence on That Side of *Tock*," *Renascence*
21, no. 4 (Summer, 1969): 207-9.
14. Ihab Hassan, *The Literature of Silence: Henry Miller and Samuel
Beckett* (New York: Alfred A. Knopf, 1967).

intention, or the reader's response—the importance of silence is that it suggests how a work can be open to something that is not less than itself, namely to those pregnant silences from which the language arises and to which it returns. Going "beyond formalism," then, to use Geoffrey Hartman's phrase,[15] need not be a relapse into expressive literary theories like Coleridge's, or affective theories like those of Sidney, Arnold, or Richards, or mimetic theories— although all of these theories have their valid points to make at times—but rather an attempt to hazard some guess about the relation between the work's language and the end towards which the language leads the reader, while not actually being that end itself.

Incidentally, a formalist critique should operate on religious expressions, too, for religious forms, like aesthetic forms, should not be made subservient to some other—moral, philosophical, psychological, or sociological—thing. But the criticism needed even more is one that will direct attention beyond forms to their subservience to the "more" to which they are intended to lead. Religion suffers either from the lack of respect for forms or from formalism. As Joseph Campbell points out, Christianity especially tends to maintain people's dependency on its forms.[16]

So much, then, for these suggested correlations between literary and religious life at the aesthetic moment of creation—the special identity, the interest in wholeness and totality, and the orientation toward silence. We turn now to the aesthetic moment of reception, to the reader.

II

Additional problems can be expected in our discussion of the aesthetic moment of reading since less theoretical work has been done on this than on the moment of the writer. Although there are current theoretical discussions of reading, there will be fewer occasions in this section than in the preceding when we can benefit from problems clarified by others or from emphases and approaches that are well established.

15. Geoffrey A. Hartman, *Beyond Formalism: Literary Essays 1958–1970* (New Haven: Yale University Press, 1970).
16. Joseph Campbell, "Bios and Mythòs: Prolegomena to a Science of Mythology," in *Myth and Literature: Contemporary Theory and Practice*, ed. John B. Vickery (Lincoln: University of Nebraska Press, 1966), p. 22.

Notice should first of all be taken of the fact that reading is a creative act, too, and the reader describes by his act a pattern similar to the artist's; the reader moves from need, through the discipline of reading, to something other or more. The reader comes to the act with some lack, some deficiency. That need is deepened, changed, or directed by the reading. And, however it is to be termed—catharsis, unity, consolation, or insight—the reader experiences the new or the other which should be adequate to the need brought to the work, a need which the work has changed. It is this consequence that Northrop Frye alludes to when he asserts that the reading of a work of literature cannot finally be only a depressing experience;[17] always to be expected is the consequence of receiving something new. Similarly, the religious parallels noted before at these points within the creative act of writing are relevant to the act of reading, namely, the sense of need, the discipline of religious forms, and fulfillment, however that is to be termed or described.

However, there are points of correlation particularly to be noted in the aesthetic moment of reading. One, for example, is the attitude of the reader before the work, an attitude which is quite unique. The reader must be receptive to the work if he is fully to enter it. As George Steiner puts it, ". . . to read well is to take great risks. It is to make vulnerable our identity, our self-possession."[18] A defensive or insecure reader forfeits the possibility of entering or of being entered. The readiness is not so much a willingness to agree as a readiness to go along.

This unusual attitude of openness closely parallels the kind of stance that is required before a religious object. A religious man is required to stand openly before the possibility of a religious object's power: "Let it be done to me according to thy word"; "Speak, Lord, for thy servant heareth." Even someone outside a religious community who wants to gain some understanding of or feeling for the power and meaning of the religious forms of that community must enter in or go along; if he brings to the encounter demands he expects to be met or preconceptions he

17. Northrop Frye, *Anatomy of Criticism* (New York: Atheneum, 1966), p. 94.
18. George Steiner, *Language and Silence: Essays on Language, Literature and the Inhuman* (New York: Atheneum, 1967), p. 10.

wants to have confirmed, his chances for entering are thereby reduced.

What the vulnerable reader is taken in by is, to put it formally, a mixture of the familiar and the strange. This seems to me a better way of describing the engaging polarities within a work, as experienced by the reader, than T. S. Eliot's traditional and individual or Leslie Fiedler's archetype and signature,[19] or any, wherever they may be, who deal with a division between matter and form, ideas and language. The new in a work is what distances, challenges, produces change and exacts effort; the familiar in it encourages, sets at ease, rewards immediately, attaches the reader to the work. The complex of the familiar and the strange acts upon the openness which a reader brings to the work.[20]

These qualities of the work which engage the reader find their religious counterparts in the category of mystery. The ambiguity in mystery is described by Rudolf Otto as the terrifying and the fascinating, more extreme words than the terms "strange" and "familiar" but appropriate words for Otto's discussion, since for him religion is nothing if not extraordinary.[21] His term, instead of mystery, is, of course, "numinous," a term denoting matters too extraordinary to be useful in pointing to that mix in literature we have referred to as the strange and the familiar. Perhaps, though, mystery is not an inappropriate word to use at certain levels for this aspect of both aesthetic and religious forms, and the word "mystery" provides us with a rare semantic occasion to point to the correlations about which we have been speaking.

A second point at which religious correlations can be drawn to the aesthetic moment of reading is in the acceptance of authority. The reader must create a reader willing to read as the implied author directs. Caroline Gordon instructs the reader "to

19. T. S. Eliot, "Tradition and the Individual Talent," in *Selected Essays*, ed. T. S. Eliot (New York: Harcourt, Brace & Co., 1950), pp. 3–11; and Leslie Fiedler, "Archetype and Signature" in *No! In Thunder* (London: Eyre and Spottiswoode, 1963), pp. 309–28.
20. On the point of openness and expectation see Eric Donald Hirsch's discussion of *vorverständis* in *Validity in Interpretation* (New Haven: Yale University Press, 1967), pp. 78–111.
21. Rudolf Otto, *The Idea of the Holy: An Inquiry into the Non-rational Factor in the Idea of the Divine and its Relation to the Rational*, trans. John W. Harvey (New York: Oxford University Press, 1958).

follow the author's footsteps,[22] and this is because a reader learns how to define the genre, as Eric Donald Hirsch would put it, only through his reading of the text, since, as David Daiches reminds us, "the novel fulfills itself in many and various ways and no single definition of a good novel will do."[23] This is not to say that the reader comes with no previous literary experience or with no genre expectations. The writer can expect such things of his reader, and previous experience and genre expectations add greatly to a work's potential force and meaning for a reader; in addition, a reader's knowledge saves the writer considerable time and effort. But even in the presence of conventions, the reader must give himself to the work's Virgil, following his footsteps even at familiar points to see the always strange direction that is being taken.

The category of authority is indispensable for the discussion of religion, even though the category can be of more or less centrality as a person moves from one religious community or tradition to another. In Protestantism since Schleiermacher, for example, the term becomes less important, although it could be argued that within Protestantism problems, and even a crisis, can develop from a diminution of authority. For from the deists through the romantics and down to the present day, there is in one way or another within Protestantism a deep suspicion of the misuse of authority, of priestcraft. It is interesting to note that there exists a corresponding crisis of authority in literature, especially in American literature.[24] Wayne Booth takes up, in his theoretical study of fiction, the problem of "the morality of impersonal narration."[25] Should the reader, for example, at least be entitled to know a narrator's or implied author's attitude toward his material? Others alert us to this situation; Irving Howe calls attention to the anarchistic emphasis of American

22. Caroline Gordon, *How to Read a Novel* (New York: Viking Press, 1957), p. 20.
23. David Daiches, *Literary Essays* (London: Oliver and Boyd, 1956), p. 183.
24. See Roy Harvey Pearce, *The Continuity of American Poetry* (Princeton: Princeton University Press, 1961).
25. Booth, *Rhetoric of Fiction*, pp. 377–98. It should also be noted that the categories of "implied" or "created" author and reader, as I have been using them in this discussion, are derived from Booth.

literature,[26] and T. S. Eliot, in his essay on "Religion and Literature," asserts that the literature of our time lacks a context of commonly held ethical norms grounded in religious belief, and that criticism, consequently, should move toward ethical and theological considerations in its judgments on literary texts.[27] The importance of authority for both religion and literature and the problems that this dimension of their lives creates need a long and fresh reappraisal, and students of both religion and literature may be able to help each other in this enterprise.

In addition to the open attitude of the reader before the literary work and his acceptance of the authority of its implied author, an additional aspect of the aesthetic moment of reading seems worthy of attention, namely, the reader's unavoidably personal involvement with the text, even in his interpretation and criticism of it. Such involvement is disdained by some critics and theorists; T. S. Eliot, for example, calls it adolescent and insists on detachment, a disinterest that is created by engagement with many different and conflicting world-views.[28] This impersonal theory of interpretation and criticism parallels his impersonal theory of poetic creation. But perhaps the critical forum would be greatly impoverished if impersonal interpretations were to be the only acceptable kind. Indeed, despite Northrop Frye's emphasis to the contrary, criticism returns to as well as arises from "the incommunicable experience."[29] However much historical relativity and subjectivism should be resisted, as E. D. Hirsch emphasizes,[30] the reader's involvement with a work is to some degree responsible for the interpretation of it that he will render. An interpreter is or is not engaged by a text, and it is not necessarily a critical virtue to expunge all trace of relationship or lack of it. This is no advocacy of polemic for its own sake in the critical forum; yet, to criticize a poem and not to be aware that it is a work with little if any current aesthetic power and mean-

---

26. Irving Howe, "Anarchy and Authority in American Literature," in *Decline of the New* (New York: Harcourt, Brace & World, 1970), pp. 97–110.
27. T. S. Eliot, "Religion and Literature," in *Selected Essays*, pp. 343–55.
28. Ibid., pp. 348–49.
29. Frye, *Anatomy of Criticism*, p. 27.
30. Hirsch, *Validity in Interpretation*.

ing, or not to be aware of the fact that to read Milton's poetry and to think lightly of his beliefs is to place on his work an aesthetic burden which it may not want to carry, is to create critical misunderstanding. Although he uses generally intelligible categories and norms, the interpreter or critic[31] is always affected by his involvement or lack of involvement in a text, and clarity in criticism could possibly be increased by more acknowledgement of that fact.

Little needs to be said to argue that religious explicators are involved in the matter about which they speak; in fact, it has been this factor in the study of religion that has created problems with its being introduced into nonconfessional settings. Although much of the interpretation and criticism of religious communities and traditions that goes on at the university level attempts to expunge traces of personal involvement with the material, the problem is not so simply solved; tolerance or pluralism or an objective study of religion can easily be masks for a loss of belief, a diminution of the importance of forms, disciplines, and authorities in religious communities which set them apart. At its worst, this attempt at impersonal interpretation can be a veiled assertion that religion is really an expression or a symptom of something else, something construed as basically sociological or psychological in nature. In fact, in such interpretation and criticism of religion, there may exist an advocacy of some kind of religion-substitute, some world-view or morality or theory of relationships which it is the intention of the interpreter subtly, even unconsciously, to introduce in the place of that religion which he has removed from his personal involvement. The problem between departments of religion and departments of literature at this point is that the one needs to be less and the other more cognizant of the personal stake present in their work and also of the resulting problems this creates for hermeneutics. A failure to recognize the situation in either case, it seems to me, is a failure to recognize the nature of the material and the increasingly intolerable separation we suffer in the academic world between our public work and our personal experiences, feelings, and beliefs.[32]

31. I follow Hirsch's distinctions in the use of these two terms.
32. This assertion, however, is no equivalent to the advocacy of religious beliefs or literary tastes in classrooms. It is a call, as I shall indicate in

Personal involvement, the acceptance of authority, and the unique attitude of openness before the work are the three aspects of the aesthetic moment of reading which I have wanted to introduce as possibly fruitful points at which mutually revealing correlations between literature and religious life and thought can be drawn. It has been my purpose in doing this, as well as in presenting similar points in the moment of creation, to suggest a supporting context for my initial assertion that narratives have real or potential religious meaning or significance because the elements of narrative, particularly when reflected upon, naturally lead to, or draw to themselves, associations or complications which are religious or religiously important. If the discussion has been able to provide such a context it is because we can see that the other two moments in the aesthetic circle besides the work itself, namely, the writing and the reading of it, also have natural associations with corresponding aspects of religious life and thought. Surely I have not drawn attention to all of the possibilities in these other two moments, and I may not have been aware of possibilities even more important than I have mentioned; but I hope that a direction for further discussion in these two areas has been indicated.

III

The preceding discussion, then, has been introductory to what now stands before us, the narrative itself. Of course, the narrative was implied throughout that discussion, and we have already indirectly pointed to many important qualities of narratives by talking about the author and the reader. We have mentioned that built into a work are images of the implied author and of the implied reader; we have discussed the orientation of a work's language toward silence; we have looked at its dominant unity-creating properties (temporal structure, metaphor, and symbol or epiphany); we have addressed the question of a work's autotelic nature as well as the polarities within it of the strange and the familiar. Now we must look at what it is in narratives that makes them, so to speak, stand by themselves, what it is in them that is not so clearly and closely connected with matters relating

---

the Conclusion, to enter a religious world, as well as a literary one, as a realm of possible religious or aesthetic power and meaning.

to the author or the reader. To put it boldly, narratives create their own power and meaning; they create author and reader just as author and reader create them. They do this by having certain properties with which the author and the reader, like it or not, have to cope. A narrative has meaning and exerts power because of and in terms of its elements. And a writer and reader should have no dealings with narrative if they have no interest in the kinds of power and meaning the elements of narrative generate. Conversely, author and reader are limited by the kinds of power and meaning which potentially reside in the elements, although, as we shall see, the elements of narrative make narrative a potentially quite comprehensive and inclusive literary form.

The elements of narrative are setting, plot, character, and tone. Of course, as in all things aesthetic, the elements in a single work are not cleanly separated from one another. They influence and determine the group and are affected in exchange. But it can generally be said that in particular works the four elements are not of equal importance, that the principal power and meaning sources of an individual narrative tend to be fewer than four, although all four are always present. When this is true, when one or two elements dominate a particular narrative, the process of isolation becomes easier.

Now it should be noted in passing that an important literary objection could be raised to this approach toward the analysis of narrative in terms of these four elements, the objection being that narratives are collections of words. There are no plots or characters or settings or tones in narratives; there is only the language by which narratives are constituted. We are too indebted to the New Critical emphasis on the primacy of literary language to take an attack like this too lightly.[33] My response to this legitimate objection is, first, that narratives, unlike lyric poems, do not, with some exceptions or except for some passages, lend themselves to close verbal analysis; second, that I shall treat language choice or style under the topic of tone; and, third and most important, that these "elements" are not presented here as though they were apart from or "beneath" fic-

33. See David Lodge, *Language and Fiction: Essays in Criticism and Verbal Analysis of the English Novel* (New York: Columbia University Press, 1966).

tional language. Quite the contrary is true. They are, instead, summary concepts, brief descriptions of what appears to be the intention of fictional language. They are elements or fiction-making characteristics in this sense: Narratives are extended verbal expressions in prose which have for their primary intention the creation of images of setting, plot, character, and tone.

The procedure which follows is simply this: First, some comments will be made about the element to which the chapter is given; then three works of fiction will be examined—works in which that particular element is dominant, in which, even, reflection on that element has led to associations or complications within the work that are recognizably religious or of religious importance; finally, in each chapter, I shall discuss briefly some aspects of contemporary religious discussion which are of a somewhat marketplace, rather than confessional, nature. It is hoped that the kind of fictions I have selected for examination will not deflect attention from the overall argument of this study, namely, that relations of the kind I am suggesting are natural to, and actually or potentially present in, all narratives. Further, by pointing to more publicly acceptable discussions in religion I do not mean to advocate them as satisfying in themselves, or, even less, as offering substitutes for more traditional theological affirmations. Rather, by coming, so to speak, out of the church and into the street, these discussions may make a connection with the kinds of considerations which the elements of narrative naturally lead to that otherwise would be absent. In the Conclusion I shall have the opportunity, in an examination of the defining characteristics of religion, to suggest indirectly what may be wanting in such discussions, helpful as, at a certain level, those discussions may be. In the Conclusion, furthermore, I shall try to summarize what I shall be suggesting in the third selection of each of the chapters, namely, that the elements of narrative are correlates of the elements of religion.

Atmosphere and Otherness

I

Much that generally is included in setting, the first element of narrative we shall consider, is actually a part of plot and character. Consequently, I have substituted the term "atmosphere" for setting, meaning by the term that aspect of setting which determines the range of possibilities or the conditions by or under which the fictional world is constituted. The atmosphere of a narrative suggests those conditions which the characters or narrator cannot change; it includes the time, place, and circumstances in which characters or narrators find themselves and with or within which they have to live or work. Although I shall be talking of these conditions of the fictional world primarily as limitations, they need not be seen as only negative. They also provide possibilities. In any case, they are there, quite apart from the characters' or narrator's ability to alter them. Atmosphere is "otherness"; it is there, and, whether they like it or not, the characters and narrator must live out their fictional lives on the stage or within the walls with which they have been provided.

Atmosphere can be less or more important in one fiction than in another. The formula, "once upon a time," suggests a narrative in which time, place, and conditions are minimal considerations. In modern fiction, however, atmosphere tends to be very important indeed, and characters and narrators not only are conscious of the conditions in which, willy-nilly, they find themselves, but also worry about those conditions and spend a considerable amount of thought and effort coming to terms with them. When that begins to happen, when characters and narrators begin to concern themselves with what it is they should do or say in the face of those forces or limits which affect and even determine their lives, they can easily be led to, or they can draw into their considerations of atmosphere, enrichments and complications of thought and response which are religiously significant. That is so because atmosphere suggests the borders of human influence, suggests that in human life which is encountered as standing beyond the reach of human influence, modification, and control. Atmosphere suggests otherness, and otherness is a religiously significant category. But before looking more fully into this matter and before looking at three works of fiction in which atmosphere is a dominant element, some general comments about the role of atmosphere in modern fiction ought to be made.

First, modern fiction is more often marked by an atmosphere which suggests limiting, than by atmosphere which suggests extending or supporting, conditions within the fictional world. Characters find themselves in worlds which tend not to grant them what they need and desire. In a word, modern fiction is marked by a negative atmosphere, and characters generally do not feel that they or their interests are supported by the circumstances in their worlds which they cannot control, or even fully understand. The first thing to be noted about atmosphere in modern fiction, then, is that it is largely responsible for the existence in our time of a mode of literature Northrop Frye calls ironic.[1]

The interest in atmosphere which marks modern literature does not separate it from the Western tradition, as a number of historical considerations will reveal. For one thing, the dominant religious traditions of the West take time and space seriously as the location of divine action or presence. Erich Auerbach emphasized this in his study of the representation of reality in Western literature, particularly in his comments on "background."[2] Although it can be said that the Bible, with its strongly monotheistic emphasis and sky orientation, tends to minimize setting, it, with but a few exceptions, affirms the religious significance of time, place, and circumstances. Again, with some notable exceptions, this emphasis continues down to the modern period. The

1. Northrop Frye, *Anatomy of Criticism* (New York: Atheneum, 1966).
2. Erich Auerbach, *Mimesis: The Representation of Reality in Western Literature* (Princeton: Princeton University Press, 1953), pp. 3–24.

Enlightenment, while responsible in some respects for alienating the mind from circumstances and, with Descartes and others, taking mind as primary, was also associated with a new reverence toward nature and history. Bliss Perry ties fictional interest in setting to Rousseau's belief that landscape is capable of forming and even of changing character, and working from Rousseau's *La nouvelle Heloise* (1761), he traces this interest in setting through English romanticism.[3] We can see this reverence of a theological kind in Tom Paine's assertion, *"The Word of God is the creation we behold,"* a belief crucial to his "age of reason," since he stands as one newly awakened to a world open to human understanding and control.[4]

In American religious and literary developments, as Tony Tanner and others have made clear, a similar response, epitomized by the term "wonder," characterizes the nineteenth century and continues down, although in modified form, to the present, so that recent writers like Percy, Updike, Malamud, Kerouac, Kesey, and even Mailer can link spiritual rejuvenation to the "otherness" of a natural world, one lying beyond the borders of human modification and control.[5]

The contemporary emphasis on the discontinuity between man and his setting, specifically the existentialist witness to the experience of the absurd, complicates this modern emphasis, in both its rationalistic and romantic forms, on man at home in this world. What characters confront in the ambience created by this emphasis is not supportive of their search for identity and value; the "other" threatens their very use of the pronoun "I". The terror of setting results in human isolation and intimidation. Atmosphere becomes discontinuous with, and even hostile to, man's deepest needs and desires.

While this emphasis on the negative quality of atmosphere in

3. Bliss Perry, *A Study of Prose Fiction* (Boston: Houghton Mifflin Co., 1902), p. 160.

4. Thomas Paine, *The Age of Reason* (New York: Bobbs-Merrill Co., 1948), pt. 1, p. 24.

5. See Tony Tanner, *The Reign of Wonder* (Cambridge: At the University Press, 1965) as well as Leo Marx, *The Machine in the Garden: Technology and the Pastoral Ideal in America* (New York: Oxford University Press, 1964); Wright Morris, *The Territory Ahead* (New York: Harcourt, Brace & Co., 1957); Irving Howe, *Decline of the New* (New York: Harcourt, Brace & World, 1970); Richard W. B. Lewis, *The American Adam* (Chicago: University of Chicago Press, 1955).

modern fiction needs to be made, it should also be pointed out that the times and places associated with youth, women, and the countryside, even in Kafka, Camus, and Sartre, are more supportive of human interest than the times and places of adulthood, men, and the city. This distinction has aesthetic as well as historical-social roots. Historically, of course, it is tied to the romantic emphasis on the spiritually supportive potential of nature and on both the primacy of the individual and his essential goodness. Consequently, any associations which suggest possibilities apart from society tend to be more supportive of personal, spiritual well being. Lionel Trilling, in his lucid study of sincerity and authenticity, reveals, for example, those points in Western intellectual history in which society, particularly urban society, began to be viewed as something other than and hostile to personal worth, as something corrosive to the sincerity of the individual person. Working with Diderot's *Le Neveu de Rameau* (1761-1774), he examines the presupposition that society does not set the range of virtues and values within which it is the actual destiny and nature of man to live.[6] This dichotomy between personal worth and social setting is particularly noticeable in American literature because of the personal freedom suggested by the break from the complexities of European culture, because of the vast natural resources at hand, and because, as Marius Bewley puts it, there is revealed by American literature of the nineteenth century "the sense that there is a world of abstract ideas and ideals, and a world of bitter fact, but no society or tradition or orthodoxy in which the two worlds can interact and qualify each other."[7]

A second reason for the distinction in value between youth-woman-countryside and adult-male-city lies in the nature of the creative act. Modern literature, as it increasingly became a vernacular literature divorced from original or revived classical

6. Lionel Trilling, *Sincerity and Authenticity* (Cambridge: Harvard University Press, 1971), particularly pp. 26–52. See also, W. H. Auden, *The Enchafèd Flood or The Romantic Iconography of the Sea* (New York: Random House, 1950) and A. Leslie Willson, *A Mythical Image: The Ideal of India in German Romanticism* (Durham, N.C.: Duke University Press, 1964), two interesting studies of the investment of meaning in kinds of settings, particularly in the latter eighteenth and nineteenth centuries.
7. Marius Bewley, *The Eccentric Design: Form in the Classic American Novel* (New York: Columbia University Press, 1959), p. 18.

roots in form and language, became so much more an affair of starting afresh. Rather than having his Aristotle, Virgil, or Horace before him, the writer, particularly in America, has a sense of starting from scratch. The aesthetic discipline of creating, then, becomes more and more a process of divestment, of seeing freshly; one thinks of the discipline of stripping down in Poe's narratives, of using nature in Emerson's early essay on the topic, of simplifying for Thoreau, of Ishmael's rejecting the stepmother society, of Huck Finn's undercutting of civilization, and even of the converting in James's novels of the complexities of social interactions at their highest and most subtle level into plots of moral evil and redemption. The aesthetic discipline, in a word, is a matter of stepping back, erasing accumulated preconceptions, speaking freshly, honestly; of such a kind are the prevailing characteristics of American writers. Leslie Fiedler, while insightful in his analysis of the proclivity of American literature to move toward boyishness, need not have given the tendency so psychological an interpretation,[8] for the return to boyhood, with its image of a son nurtured by nature and its emphasis on male friendship, is also a simulation of the aesthetic discipline behind much of this literature, namely, the aesthetic discipline of starting anew.

In addition to these general historical or cultural remarks about the role of setting in modern literature, I would like to draw attention in concluding this section to some formal literary consequences of the important part played by atmosphere in modern literature. The first of these consequences is that atmosphere often assumes the role of the antagonist. It has often been noted that modern fiction is marked by the reduction of the protagonist, the vanishing hero, the exile, the awkward outsider, or pariah. The representative characters of recent literature are not greater than or even equal to ourselves but less than we are, inhabitants of what Northrop Frye calls the winter world of the literary cycle. But it is not so often noticed as it should be that tied to this phenomenon is the loss of a personal antagonist. What characters are usually up against is not a worthy human

8. See Leslie Fiedler, *An End to Innocence* (Boston: Beacon Press, 1955), and idem, *Love and Death in the American Novel* (New York: Criterion Books, 1960).

opponent but some impersonal, even antihuman power. Before an identifiable and human antagonist a character can actualize his potential, but an indefinite, pervasive, and unalterable set of severely limiting conditions tends to reduce human life and even to threaten its worth and viability.

Another formal consequence of heavy atmosphere is rhetorical in nature. The rhetorical use or consequence of atmosphere seems to escape critical notice, since it is so generally assumed that the rise in importance of this element is a result of artists' interest in telling us something about the world in which we live, such as God's death, the world's broken center, or social evil and violence. But it should also be noticed that the creation of an effective image of negative atmosphere can, at the same time, create between the implied author and implied reader a sense that they share a set of circumstances and have, consequently, something in common. Particularly is this true when the circumstances are hostile. There is a bit of a football cheer about the cry, "It is against us, therefore we are together." "They're out there!" begins Ken Kesey's *One Flew Over the Cuckoo's Nest.* If a sense of a common situation of loss, crisis, or threat can be created by an author or narrator, he can encourage the reader's identification with him as someone similarly distressed. A "we are in this together" association of survival results. In fact, something that seems to unify twentieth century Western literature is the collective image it has provided of a world in which people live at considerable risk to their physical, mental, moral, and, even more, spiritual well being—an image of the conditions of life as a situation of stress which we share in common.

A final formal matter—and I shall have more to say of this later—is that the mimetic consequence of the image of atmosphere in modern literature is not so much to reflect specific conditions in our world—violence, immoral society, or disunification—but, rather, to reflect a more general quality of human life, namely, that it is limited. The mimetic consequence of the use of atmosphere in rather recent narrative is an image of human life as limited by, and needing to come to terms with, otherness. The collective image of atmosphere in recent narrative is of a general otherness which marks the boundaries, awareness of which helps to define human life.

II

By selecting Albert Camus' *The Plague,* Pär Lagerkvist's *The Sibyl,* and Heinrich Böll's *The Clown* as examples of fiction in which atmosphere is a dominant element, in which characters or narrators are aware of atmosphere, and in which their reflection on atmosphere leads them to religious or religiously important considerations, I do not intend to limit fiction of this kind to the Continent. Preoccupation with atmosphere is widespread, and, as Chester E. Eisinger put it, "Americans were trying to meet in literature the same dangers to the existence of man as man that Europeans were meeting in philosophy, and, Americans were reaching, more or less independent of Europeans, similar conclusions."[9] But we tend to identify the preoccupation with otherness, particularly of unalterable conditions that are hostile to human life, with Continental thought and literature, and what can be detected there can be seen by inference to be relevant to the wider literary scene.

That atmosphere, the critical situation created in Oran by the disease, is a dominant element in *The Plague* need not be argued. The citizens of this town have their lives determined by the conditions which prevail, if only because they are locked into the situation. The principal action of the narrative deals with the process of people responding to or coming to terms with the desperate conditions of their lives. The plot of the work is primarily determined by the plague itself, the narrative beginning with its appearance and ending with its retreat. Characters develop not because they change, but because the critical situation in which they live provides a pressure under which the characters are stripped down to their true identities, reveal themselves or are revealed to be what they actually are, and provide the reader with perspectives from which the plague is viewed. Similarly, tone is determined by the plague, by the need to bring it clearly into view and to describe kinds of human responses to it. These formal characteristics of *The Plague* make it, with the other narratives discussed in this section, an example of what is beginning to be referred to as the "spatial" novel.[10]

9. Chester E. Eisinger, *Fiction of the Forties* (Chicago: University of Chicago Press, 1967), p. 309.
10. See, e.g., Sharon Spencer, *Space, Time and Structure in the Modern Novel* (New York: New York University Press, 1971).

Equally clear is the fact that the characters are aware of the conditions in their city which are so determinative of their lives and which, try as they initially may, they cannot actually alter. They think and talk about the atmosphere, and these reflections and conversations take on a religious quality primarily with Father Paneloux—his sermons, his personal resolution of the problem of suffering, and his conversations with Rieux. While the more religious and theological response of Paneloux to the plague is presented by the narrator as simply another kind of response—along with the panic and despair of the majority of the citizens, the simple acceptance of M. Othon, Cottard's affirmation of calamity, the distance of the asthma patient and Rieux's mother from the plague, Rambert's attempts to flee it, the quiet opposition of Grand and Castel to the plague, and, most importantly, Rieux's clear-sightedness and relentless resistance of it—the priest's attempt to come to terms with the situation is brought into direct relation to the more favored responses of Rieux and Tarrou through Paneloux's presence at the death of Othon's son and the force of Paneloux's integrity, seen most of all in his refusal of medical aid for himself. Indeed, it can be said that Rieux's faith in something worth affirming about human life and Tarrou's program of secular sainthood gain visibility in their juxtaposition to Paneloux's specifically theological understandings and religious attitudes toward the crisis.

While Rieux takes seriously Paneloux's interpretation of the conditions of their common life under the plague, he establishes his own response in opposition to Christian belief. Rather than affirm the power and reality of something other behind the terrible limiter of human life which the plague becomes, Rieux takes that limit as absolute. But the border of human understanding and control delineated by the presence of the plague allows, too, a clear understanding of, and appreciation for, what it means to be human. By resisting the plague, by saying no, the pronoun "I" is established. Identity arises in the process of defending the sanctity of the self against whatever in life disregards it. In the same process a person becomes aware not only of his own self but also of what it means to be human, and, when people similarly conscious of their situation do this in consort, the human community is created. A person comes to know what it means to be human in the face of whatever it may be that calls the viability of the human into question, that creates consciousness of the limits of human understanding and control.

The plague, then, is a limiter, a disvalue which clarifies the borders of human life, an image of otherness which the characters, particularly Rieux, must acknowledge as irrevocably there. In addition, and in relation to the plague, other limiters are suggested—bureaucracy, oppressive weather, physical separation from loved ones, earthquakes, old age. Oran is a microcosm, while the plague and other disvalues suggest what is permanently and universally limiting to human life; the result is that the atmosphere of *The Plague* is an image of that otherness encountered in human life by which life is absolutely and universally limited.

Tarrou adds an important dimension to this image of atmosphere. The experience of the citizens of Oran brings into focus those natural conditions which limit human life; but Tarrou is aware, also, that personal and social immorality and evil limit and threaten the viability of personal identity and integrity as well. He has reached the conclusion that society, inevitably and universally, limits and destroys individual human life in society's processes of self-preservation and advancement. Consequently, Tarrou finds it perfectly consistent to withdraw from contact with people and finally to retreat into death. While Paneloux is a religious ascetic, withdrawing from and rejecting this world in favor of some other hidden one, Tarrou is a secular ascetic who, similar to Rieux's mother and the asthma patient, rejects a society which destroys the present and the individual for the sake of the future and the collective. Rieux, following neither of these men, grounds his rebellion in the conviction that human life, awakened by a consciousness of what in the world opposes life, is a viable and valuable reality.

In *The Plague,* then, with all else that it is and that could be said about it, we have a narrative presided over by an image of atmosphere. The principal intention of the narrator is to bring that atmosphere into view, to depict kinds of human responses to it, and, indirectly, to advocate his own evaluation of the relation of the absolute and universal limits of human life to the process of developing self-awareness. The narrator and the character are conscious of those conditions in their world which set the limits of their lives, they reflect on those conditions, and they extend their conversations to a point at which conclusions are drawn and decisions made which are religious or religiously important. Enrichments and complications of the image of atmosphere lead naturally to religious or religiously important discussions of otherness, absolute limiters, and eschatology.

Heinrich Böll's *The Clown* makes central an image of atmosphere which it is Tarrou's purpose to contribute to in *The Plague,* namely, otherness and limitation as social and moral evil. The image of atmosphere in this narrative is postwar German society. Hans Schier's experiences in that society create for him simultaneously the understandings that society is a force which is antithetically related to his deepest desires and values and that he must find some way to be human despite that force.

Contemporary German society, for one thing, is obsessed with abstractions, titles, prestige, and social acceptance. An orientation to abstraction injures and even kills relationships and attitudes of real human worth. Marie ends her relationship with Hans after seven years of intimacy because of the pressure of high ranking clerics whose social prestige Marie admired. The church, then, is interested in nothing so much as in its own institutional visibility and advancement. The same kind of attitude accounts for the readiness of people to put themselves into distinguishing organizations rather than into real relations with other individuals. Schier's mother does not realize that her participation as executive committee president of The Societies for Reconciliation of Racial Differences is divisive. Kostert is head of the Christian Educational Society, an affiliation which does not seem to hinder his ability to cheat Hans out of his earnings. And Marie participates in group discussions held by affluent Catholics on the topics of spiritual discipline and the self-denying contributions made to society and the church by saints. This orientation to abstraction, this love of prestige, title, and affiliation, arises from and produces hypocrisy, self-deception, and self-aggrandizement.

In addition, Hans judges contemporary German society to be schizophrenic, particularly in its capacity to repress its violent history. This repression is both the cause and the consequence of the prevailing passion for abstraction. Concrete and little things remind people of their continuity with their circumstances, and the circumstances are continuous with the recent past—the betrayals, deceptions, and terrors of the war. Hans, in contrast, is well aware of little things and very aware of the past. He remembers his sister's death, and he recalls vividly the consequences that came to him for calling a Hitler Youth leader a Nazi "swine." Even more painful to remember is his mother's acceptance of Nazi propaganda and her readiness to accept for its sake assaults on her children. She continues this pattern by forgetting her daughter and rejecting her son.

Böll's clown works from particular limiting experiences in his relation to people to the general conclusion that his life is being opposed by the entire situation. This atmosphere becomes for him, first of all and as with Rieux, something to resist, which he does primarily by refusing to be placed in the groups and categories into which people want to put him. A second way he resists it is by being a clown; in his comic routines he can try to draw the attention of people to their own concreteness, both by masking himself and by reflecting their manners in an exaggerated way.

During the evening in Bonn which he narrates, Hans comes to the conclusion that a more radical response to the atmosphere in which he finds himself is needed. He reaches this conclusion because he finds nothing or no individual with whom he can make a connection. People he thought were close to him, members of his family and friends, are unavailable, are out of touch: Marie is with her Catholic husband in Rome; his brother Leo has been absorbed by the abstractions of the church; Edgar, who resisted abstractions, is somewhere in India or Thailand; and Heinrich, the liberal priest, left it all and ran off with a girl. The more radical response which Hans chooses is to go to that symbol of abstracted connections, the train station—a place that is absurd by being only an arbitrary point between conjunctions—to await, as a clown, little acts of charity.

By making this move Hans both rejects the society which threatens him and relates himself to little, concrete moments from his past. Chief among these moments is his relation with his sister Henrietta. Given to sudden, mystical departures, she was a girl oriented to what she called "nothing." This peculiar orientation and her sudden departures came naturally to her;

Hans had to work to achieve anything like them. He played parchisi with Marie for hours as a discipline creating that hollow center, and he had achieved something like it, too, by performing his comic routines over and over. Another concrete moment Hans likes to recall is his brother's ecstatic desire to saw wood with him, the two of them working together. The whim at the time struck Hans as arbitrary, but ten years later, in a class discussion of Lessing, he understood and began making rocking motions. These concrete moments are no less fundamental to life for the fact of being spiritual in character. They are firm, and by taking his position in relation to them rather than in those social realities that are no more than abstractions built on repression, Hans is able to make contact with something that is life-giving.

That Hans's final response to the conditions of his situation is a spiritual and even religious one is suggested, too, by the fact that although he rejects the attitudes of its leaders he does not reject the faith of the church. He spies the old clown in Pope John and wishes he could speak with him; his favorite music is the *Tantum Ergo* and the *Litany of Loretta*.

Finally, it is significant that Hans makes his radical response to the atmosphere in which he lives during Fashing, the time of carnival before Lent. When the others are finished with it, Hans will go on with the discipline of being a clown during Lent, waiting for whatever personal consequences the discipline of Lent may have for him. Rather than participate in society's rituals of departing and arriving and making abstracted connections, and even rather than participate in its rituals of Fashing and Lent, Hans makes his connection with religious time through his discipline of waiting.

The image of atmosphere in *The Clown,* then, is different from that in *The Plague.* The boundaries of individual human life are imposed by the structures and attitudes which people, because of the society by which they are absorbed, assume and maintain. The response, though one of resistance as with Rieux, is more spiritual, even religious. Hans moves toward realities of a less visible but yet more concrete status to provide for him the possibility of making a connection which, unlike travel and phone calls, will grant viability to the rooted self.

The Sibyl develops the image of atmosphere through the experiences of limitation the two principal narrators have had, experiences which are directly related to religious contexts and language. The borders which they have encountered are more spiritually construed and religiously interpreted in this work of fiction than are corresponding borders in either of the other works we have seen.

The man, a wandering Jew, called Ahasuerus in the next volume of the quartet, has sought out the sibyl because he wants to know what the future holds for him. He is anxious about the future because a curse has robbed him of the sense of an end to his life, has infinitely extended his time. Consequently, the limitless time in which he wanders has become a dreary, unmarked expanse. The complicating matter in his experience is that he has been confronted by an ultimate limiter—the curse—which has robbed him of those specific and human limitations, such as the certainty of dying, which, by implication, make life tolerable and coherent because they relate time to an ending.

In response, the sibyl recounts her personal experience on the borderline between her own feelings, understanding, and control and what lies beyond them. Her story is neatly arranged in episodes: her homelife in the country, her election as pythia, her first performance during the great festival, her experience as a a priestess, her mother's death, the one-armed man, her pregnancy and resulting expulsion from Delphi, and her life on the mountain. But more importantly, these episodes of her life cluster around three more fundamental moments: the ordinary religion of her parents and homelife, the extraordinary religion which she participated in as priestess in the temple, and her ambiguous existence on the mountainside since leaving the temple, a period of time which has characteristics of both of the other two moments. It is the tension between these former two moments, epitomized by her love with the one-armed man in the first and her spiritual-sexual fulfillment of the pit in the second, which is held during the third moment and resolved at the end of her narration.

The principal structural tensions of the two confessions and the three moments of the sibyl's life are supported by an array of contraries within the work: death and birth, dark and light, height and depth, kinds of animals, the two sons of God, kinds of water or dampness, city and country, pilgrims to Delphi and the wandering Jew. This mobile-like structure casts attention on the narrative's reconciliation of at least one of the major tensions, the relation of the sibyl's earlier and later lives.

The atmosphere of the sibyl's early homelife was one supportive of human life and interests. Human life, natural processes, and divine power were felt, by her parents, to be comtiguous if not continuous with one another. Although they experienced hardships, her parents lived at home in an atmosphere supportive of their lives, and they gave recognition to these forces through their simple sacrifices at the tree and spring. Even her mother's death does not threaten this understanding of the conditions of life; rather than an assault, dying is a natural process, and the mother's life is absorbed by larger natural processes.

The otherness the sibyl encounters in the pit, of course, is quite contrary to the supportive, natural-divine forces of her home. Divinity here is unnatural; violence, discontinuity, and unpredictability mark that which lies beyond her understanding and control. The power she confronts in the pit is extraordinary to human life, even disruptive to it, antithetical. Although she can put herself into position to encounter this otherness, the relationship is determined wholly by it and not by her. She is used by it, abused by it, and, when she enters desiring the encounter, she is left waiting in vain. In both religions—the one ordinary, natural, and marked by continuity; the other extraordinary, unnatural, and marked by discontinuity—death, sexuality, and life are significant components, but in the religion of the pit, death dominates and intimidates life while sexuality is violent and grotesque.

By defying the god of the pit through her affair with the one-armed man, the sibyl takes the tensions between these two religions into herself. On the mountainside she lives an ordinary life, supported by nature, continuous with her environment, aided by the goats. But qualities of the extraordinary are disruptingly present, too, first in the gestation of the child and then in its nature as an idiot.

During and after her confession to the Jew the sibyl appears to recognize the relation of the two earlier moments of her life to one another. The son is recognized as synthesizing and transcending the contraries of her home and the pit. By being more and not less than human, he takes the contraries into himself— the natural and the unnatural, the peaceful and the violent quali- ties of otherness. Her son, by his ascension, appears to transcend both her former experiences—life supported and fulfilled by divine forces and human life intimidated and manipulated by contact with the divine.

In contrast to the sibyl, the wandering Jew cannot experience the unification of his peaceful homelife and the violence com- mitted against his life as a result of the curse. He lives on with these contradictory parts. But it is possible to infer that because of the sibyl's recognition he is put into a position that will even- tually alter his present resentment and despair. This change seems complete in *The Death of Ahasuerus* when he realizes that the perpetrator of the curse was not the man he confronted but the power under which that man lived.

As in *The Plague* and *The Clown,* atmosphere is the domi- nant element of this narrative, but in *The Sibyl* the conditions of life are more supportive of the characters' needs and desires. Although there are such supportive conditions in *The Plague* as well, such as the sea and friendships, and although they become more important in *The Clown,* particularly as a time in which the waiting clown can be rooted, the conditions of life in *The Sibyl* are in the end humanly beneficial. The ascension of the sibyl's son suggests the possibility that the nonhuman and even antihuman powers of otherness which lie beyond the boundaries of human understanding and control result not only in human limitation and intimidation, but also in a human alteration which leads to greater depth or elevation. The borders of human un- derstanding and control mark regions of otherness by which human life can be infinitely expanded, not in the dreary, con- tentless way by which the wandering Jew's time has been made a limitless wasteland, but in the creative way the sibyl has al- lowed otherness completely to alter her understanding and expectations of her world.

III

Now that we have looked briefly at instances in which at- mosphere is a major or even dominant power and meaning source in each of three narratives—narratives in which charac-

ters or narrators are aware of atmosphere, think about or react
to it, and in which these reflections and actions are religiously
significant—it becomes necessary to say what it is about atmosphere that brings to it rather naturally enrichments and
complications which have these religious qualities. What, in
other words, do categories like "conditions of life," "otherness,"
and "limiters" have to do with religion?

The point of connection lies here: Atmosphere is an image
within a narrative of possibilities or powers which lie beyond
the borders of human alteration, understanding, and control,
and a religious man is a person who, among other things, is
primarily oriented to what lies beyond human understanding
and control. Whatever realm or possibility is suggested by the
phrase "beyond human understanding and control" can be hypothesized as a common ground, however imprecisely marked, between religion and a narrative, common ground on which they
can move toward one another. The phrase suggests an area of
possibility toward which reflection on atmosphere within a fiction can easily lead, and it is a phrase that could be used in the
marketplace, so to speak, to explain what it is to which a
religious man is primarily oriented.

"Otherness" can be used as a term suggesting the fairly enigmatic instance of becoming conscious of or confronting some
aspect, dimension, or quality of one's world as marked by
nothing so much as its permanent, categorical resistance to
human understanding and control. Otherness is "beyond human
understanding and control" confronted as forcefully intransigent.
"Otherness" suggests, therefore, a kind of fictional atmosphere,
and it represents a kind of marketplace translation of the religious categories of "holy" or "divine."

We should trace for a moment the line of thought that leads
from reflection on the conditions of life to the category of
"otherness." Why should reflection by a person on the fact that
he lives at this and not some other time or in this and not some
other place lead to something religiously suggestive? To understand this process it must first be said that a person primarily
becomes aware of that in his life that lies beyond his understanding and control, of that which marks the boundaries of his
world, when he encounters the boundary as a limiter. A person
becomes aware of the walls within which he lives when he bumps

into them. When he wants to keep on living but knows that he will die, when he wants to finish writing a book but is hampered by the flu, when he wants to be in two places at once, when he wants someone to understand and trust him but learns that his motives are misunderstood, then he runs into those walls, the limits of our worlds which awaken us to the fact that there is so much to our lives that is both fundamentally important and yet beyond our understanding and control. Although we may at times also recognize how our lives are supported and enriched by what lies beyond those borders, we seem largely to become aware of otherness by encountering limiters. We have seen experiences of this kind rendered in the three fictions at which we looked. The characters have all had their lives sharply reconstituted by having confronted conditions which mark the boundaries of what they are able to understand and control. And they have become aware of otherness by encountering the conditions of their lives, at least initially, as limiters.

Confrontation with, reflection on, and response to that in life which is beyond understanding and control should not by itself be called religious. But the more a character or narrator becomes aware of otherness, the more he allows it to preoccupy him, the more oriented he becomes to it, the more it displaces in power and worth what he *can* understand and control, the more he becomes like a religious person, at least at this point, for a religious person is, as I shall be saying in my Conclusion, a person who should be understood, among other things, as one for whom, to use a marketplace expression, the transcendent is primary.

This last phrase brings us to consider briefly a few of those philosophers and theologians who, in the marketplace, directly address the religiously significant qualities of the general experience of limiters and otherness. Karl Jaspers, for example, calls limiters *Grenzsituationen,* and he defines them as

> situations such as these, namely, always being in a particular place and time, being unable to exist without struggles and suffering, experiencing unavoidable guilt, and having to die. . . .[11]

The boundaries or limiters within a person's situation confront

---

11. Karl Jaspers, *Philosophie* (Berlin, Göttingen, and Heidelberg: Springer-Verlag, 1948), pp. 469–70.

him as universal and absolute. They constitute the walls within which he must live. These borders cannot be explained in terms of something else; they are elemental to a person's existence and to his understanding of it.[12] However, for Jaspers, despite and even because of these boundaries, at the fringes of a person's understanding and control he also becomes aware of the fact that he himself, other persons, and things are supported by a kind of gratuitous housing, what Jaspers calls *Das Umgreifende*. This supportive ground which he hypothesizes beyond the fringes of our understanding and control is the source and object of what he calls philosophical faith.[13]

In this country, Professor Gordon Kaufman has construed the relation of limiters to religious faith in a similar way. He suggests a kind of spiritual discipline by which a person moves from the awareness of specific limiters to the awareness that human life can be understood primarily as arising from the consciousness of absolute and universal limitation, of ultimate limiters.[14] Since this discipline is formally similar to a traditional discipline of meditation on sin and grace[15] but without the personal dimensions provided by those traditional categories, Kaufman, by wanting to suggest a more personal or religious orientation to ultimate limits than did Jaspers, uses the finite limiter of personal encounter as providing the most interesting analogue for understanding the experience of ultimate limitation, an experience which is construed, then, as a confrontation with ultimate freedom and will.

Otherness as suggestive of aesthetic and religious dimensions of experience which lie related to but beyond a person's understanding and control is suggested in the widely influential thought of Martin Buber.[16] Although it is not altogether clear in his work what relation human intention has to the I-Thou experience, and although it is not altogether clear on what basis he

12. Ibid., pp. 471–512.

13. Karl Jaspers, *The Perennial Scope of Philosophy*, trans. Ralph Manheim (New York: Philosophical Library, 1949), p. 9.

14. Gordon Kaufman, *God the Problem* (Cambridge: Harvard University Press, 1972), particularly pp. 41–71.

15. See, e.g., Bernard of Clairvaux, *De Gradibus Humilitatis et Superbiae*, ed. Barton R. V. Mills, Cambridge Patristic Texts (Cambridge: At the University Press, 1926).

16. See Martin Buber, *I and Thou*, trans. Ronald Gregor Smith (New York: Charles Scribner's Sons, 1958).

can assert the presence of the Eternal Thou hovering at the fringes of each I-Thou relationship, Buber's holistic and somewhat mystical formulation of the religious implications of a supportive and generally shared aesthetic-spiritual experience gathers force in his discussion and continues to have consequences for any attempt to speak about the religious importance of an experience of otherness. Further, Robert N. Bellah in a recent essay describes three kinds of experiences of otherness: "overagainstness" of one's own internal life, "overagainstness" of social and historical reality, and "overagainstness" of the totality of components which constitute a person's world. Aesthetic-spiritual activity arises out of our consciousness of these various areas of experience which confront us as beyond our understanding and control, and the symbols which people create and use in order to indicate or to come to terms with these kinds of otherness arise from and support a kind of religious faith.[17]

One other kind of approach to these matters should, in conclusion, be indicated, namely, Paul Van Buren's suggestive discussion of the experience of limitation in our use of language. I shall have more to say about the limitation of language later on, but Van Buren suggests that language is inadequate to our experiences. Consequently, words like "God" can be seen as having force and meaning when they are understood as words we use whenever we are up against the final limit of what we can say about the object of our concern.[18]

Much more could be said about attempts to clarify the experience of limitation, of otherness, and its implications for religious thought and experience. Here have been suggested only some ways of moving from reflection on the conditions of life to statements concerning one's relation to that which lies beyond his understanding and control. That such statements are relevant to and lead directly to discussions of religious belief has by now, it is hoped, been made clear. That a distinction should be made between them and the basic orientation of a religious

17. Robert N. Bellah, "Transcendence in Contemporary Piety," in *Transcendence*, ed. Herbert Richardson and Donald Cutler (Boston: Beacon Press, 1969), pp. 85–97.
18. Paul M. Van Buren, *The Edges of Language: An Essay in the Logic of Religion* (New York: Macmillan Co., 1972), p. 135.

person will be reaffirmed in my Conclusion. The purpose of this chapter has been simply to clarify the status and roles of setting or atmosphere in modern narrative, to discuss some examples of fiction in which setting or atmosphere is a dominant element, and to suggest why reflection on atmosphere leads naturally to discussions that have significant religious implications. One answer to the question, Why do narratives have religious meaning?, then, is that they do because one of the elements of narrative—atmosphere—is naturally related to the experience of limitation and otherness, and limitation and otherness very easily lead to an awareness of what lies beyond human understanding and control; the phrase "what lies beyond human understanding and control" is a marketplace translation of that toward which a religious person is primarily oriented.

2.

Character and Paradigm

I

As the image of atmosphere in a narrative gathers to itself suggestions of what lies beyond human understanding and control, character in narrative is an image primarily of the potential of human consciousness to know and to manage the world in which it finds itself. The rise of the modern novel, as we shall be suggesting later on, and the high evaluation of human consciousness since the Enlightenment have much to do with one another. Character in narrative is an image of human possibilities, either for good and creativity or for evil and destruction, and the rise of modern narrative is very much tied to the effort to explore or to render paradigms of those possibilities.

When character dominates a narrative, as it so often does, the element is naturally complicated and enriched by explorations into or implicit or explicit affirmations of what the human is or can be. It is for this reason that a recent study of fictional characters can entertain them "not as figures in a fiction but as images of man."[1] What is at stake in the discussion now before us is the way in which the element of character in narrative naturally becomes an image of human possibilities or a paradigm of human potential.

This phenomenon can be detected in the way character so often is taken as naturally and inevitably the authoritative power and meaning center of a fiction. W. J. Harvey,[2] for example,

1. Vida E. Marković, *The Changing Face: Disintegration of Personality in the Twentieth-Century British Novel, 1900–1950* (Carbondale: Southern Illinois University Press, 1970), p. xv.
2. William J. Harvey, *Character and the Novel* (Ithaca, N.Y.: Cornell University Press, 1965).

argues that character is always the principal element of fiction and, more importantly, that the critic's interpretation and judgment of a novel arise from his movement between the image of man suggested by character in a fiction and the critic's own knowledge and experience of people in daily life. The power and worth of a fiction are to be determined both by the continuity between characters in fiction and our knowledge of what human beings are and by a revealing discontinuity between them; the two, fictional characters and people as we know and study them, illuminate each other. Harvey quotes approvingly C. S. Lewis's response to fiction as an experience of revelation into human nature provided by character: "This is what life is like."[3] Fictions have power and meaning because characters provide us with paradigms that illuminate the human potential for good and evil.

While Harvey construes the paradigmatic potential of character more publicly or sociologically, Scholes and Kellogg do so more personally and psychologically. This is because point of view is so central an element to their understanding of narrative. But point of view is determined, they believe, primarily by the question of how to reveal dimensions of character. The result is to tie character depiction to the author. Authors not only establish point of view in terms of necessities placed on them by their desire to reveal some kind or some dimensions of character, but they also

> tend to put themselves into their characters, and, conversely, to find in themselves an extraordinary range of dramatic possibilities, made up of aspirations, suppressed desires, masks and anti-masks, nobility and depravity.[4]

A great fiction writer is a person who creates memorable characters "from facets of the artist's psyche."[5] But whether the matter is construed sociologically as with Harvey or psychologically as with Scholes and Kellogg, the consequences are similar: Fiction is to be interpreted and judged in terms of characters as paradigms of human possibilities.

3. Ibid., p. 16.
4. Robert Scholes and Robert Kellogg, *The Nature of Narrative* (New York: Oxford University Press, 1966), p. 191.
5. Ibid., p. 192.

A literary objection to this approach to narrative will, of course, be raised by the neo-Aristotelians for whom character is an element of narrative subservient to plot. To Ronald S. Crane, for example, it is plot which makes the dramatic whole, and character, with thought and situation, are what plot orders or is ordered around.[6] Elder Olson states the matter very clearly:

> We have decided that plot governs character. This is the reverse of the relation between character and action as these occur in life; in life it is generally character which governs action. I suppose a natural instance which is more clearly parallel to what we are considering is that of finding someone who can occupy a given position or handle a particular job. When an executive has a position to fill, the job is the first consideration, and the man to hire is second. . . . Similarly, if certain actions are to happen in the plot, and produce a given effect, a character must be invented or found who can perform them.[7]

Although for the neo-Aristotelians character in narrative can have important mimetic consequences, it is always found in narrative as subjected to the principal aesthetic factor, namely, plot.

Another literary objection to the widespread tendency to take character as the dominant element of fiction and to interpret and judge characters as paradigms of human possibilities comes from theorists oriented to the New Criticism. The power and meaning of a narrative for such theorists would arise from the presence of voice within a fiction—the way of speaking, a way not like ordinary ways, surely, and not like the way of speaking in some other work of literature. David Lodge says, for example:

> The closer we get to defining the unique identity and interest of *this* plot, of *that* character, the closer we are brought to a consideration of the language in which we encounter these things.[8]

At one level Professor Lodge is arguing for the primacy of language in a fiction. But his argument goes beyond that. Like any-

6. See Ronald S. Crane, "The Concept of Plot and the Plot of Tom Jones," in Ronald S. Crane, ed., *Critics and Criticism*, abridged ed. (Chicago: University of Chicago Press, 1957), particularly pp. 66–67.
7. Elder Olson, *Tragedy and the Theory of Drama* (Detroit: Wayne State University Press, 1961), p. 79.
8. David Lodge, *Language and Fiction: Essays in Criticism and Verbal Analysis of the English Novel* (New York: Columbia University Press, 1966), p. 78.

one oriented to the New Criticism, he prizes what I shall describe as tone in narrative in chapter 4. That is, character is not so important an element of narrative as is the unique use of language by which it is constituted, a use that suggests a particular experience within it—the enclosure by language of a new arena of significant possibility.

Although I shall want to return to the neo-Aristotelians in my chapter on plot and to the New Criticism in my chapter on tone, I want now to suggest that this argument can be settled in the following ways. First, it is mistaken to assert in an a priori way that one of the elements of narrative always will be dominant. While startling advances can be made in narrative theory by emphasizing one of narrative's elements in this way, the insights thereby gained are eventually offset by the confusion which results when such an emphasis encounters a discussion which presumes or argues that one of the other elements is always and necessarily primary in a fiction. Second, it may be possible to suggest that when critics emphasize character and interpret and judge narrative in terms of character as an image of human possibilities, they are viewing character at, let us say, a different level from theorists who see character's relation to, even subservience to, other elements. And while what follows about levels of meaning in the element of character could be applied also to the images of atmosphere, plot, and tone in a narrative, they apply most naturally to character because of the way in which character tends to be enriched and complicated in meaning within a narrative, namely, as an image of human potential.

There are, let us remind ourselves, four levels from and at which the power and meaning of character can be generated and expanded.[9] The first of these is the literal level. Character at this level gathers power and meaning to itself through its organic relation to the other fictional elements. Character has its power and meaning in relation to its setting, to the temporal movement of the work, and to the subjective presence or tone. Character is

---

9. See William F. Lynch, *Christ and Apollo: The Dimensions of the Literary Imagination* (New York: New American Library, 1963), pp. 220–54 and St. Thomas Aquinas, *Summa Theologiae* (London: Eyre and Spottiswoode, 1964), vol. 1, article 10, "Whether Its Sacred Writings Are to be Interpreted in Several Senses," pp. 37–41.

rooted in relations with the other elements at this level, and when it has limited import as a paradigm of human possibilities in a particular narrative it is because one or more of the other elements is drawing attention to itself. For this reason, conversely, character is most easily a paradigm of human possibilities in parables or in formula stories like the lives of saints, since in them the other narrative elements have been stylized according to formula. Character, though, always operates at least at this level, and even when it can be judged the most important element in a particular narrative it should be understood first of all in its organic relation to the other elements. This is the level at which Lodge and Olson are considering character.

The second way in which a character can generate power and assume meaning is through his relation to extraliterary counterparts in history, society, or individual personality. A character at this level is significant not only because of the place he holds in the fictional world of which he is a part but also because he illuminates what people are like in real life or what they are like under certain circumstances. It is to character at this level that the remarks mentioned before from Harvey, Scholes and Kellogg, and C. S. Lewis refer: "This is what people are like!" The appropriate term from the fourfold hermeneutic is "allegorical." This term should not be taken as referring to a one-one relation between characters and separate, actual people, ideas, or human types, traits, virtues or vices—that would be a special use of character at this level. Rather, it refers to all relations of character to the world outside the fiction, from which relation character can take on power and meaning.

Vida Markovíc, with whom I began this chapter, moves, as do others, from this second level to a third level at which character can generate power and gather meaning. Here character arises above not only its literary context, but also its historical and social references to reveal something new about human possibilities. Here character becomes paradigmatic of some style, problem, perversity, or virtue. Here something about human potential is epitomized; Don Quixote, Captain Ahab, Rupert Birkin, or Holden Caulfield stand above their literary and their historical-social context and bring to focus or establish an image of something unique, new, or revealing about the human person. This is character functioning at the "anagogical" level.

The fourth level is "tropological," and it tends, as we shall be seeing later on, to be used infrequently in modern narrative. At this level, character is powerful and meaningful because it opens up to something beyond itself, something which by its durability, inclusiveness, or depth is more than individual while yet inescapably related to human possibility. D. H. Lawrence develops some of his characters in this direction, such as Paul Morel in *Sons and Lovers* or Ursula Brangwen in *The Rainbow;* Hermann Hesse's Demian or Siddhartha are developed by him in this way, too. Or we may see some of Faulkner's women suggesting a point of transition between the human and something more than human by which the human is elevated and expanded or from which it can draw in order to endure—Dilsey, Lena Grove, or even Eula Varner.

It is in the process of actualizing possible meanings at these levels that character becomes a dominant element in a narrative and, as it increasingly does so, becomes paradigmatic for human nature as it is, could, or even should, or should not be. The position character gains as it becomes important in a narrative is religiously suggestive because character as paradigm takes on a kind of exemplary and even revealing role, one similar to the force felt by a religious community from its authoritative figures.

Before returning to a discussion of what it is about human life that modern characters reveal, we should look at three fictions in which character is the dominant element, in which the element is developed along the levels suggested above, and in which human possibilities rendered in character are complicated and enriched with religious associations. Furthermore, these three examples, Graham Greene's *A Burnt-Out Case,* Isaac Singer's *The Magician of Lublin,* and Flannery O'Connor's *The Violent Bear It Away* are helpful to the discussion because they present to us characters whose problems arise because they have adopted paradigms of human possibilities which dominate the Western, post-Enlightenment tradition and are found to be inadequate. Looking at these fictions, then, will put us into a position from which we can examine briefly the spiritual investment of modern narrative in character and end the chapter by indicating current awareness of the religious significance of secular paradigms of human possibilities.

II

Although, as in all of Greene's novels, atmosphere is heavy in *A Burnt-Out Case,* it serves character by putting pressure on it. Character, as an image first of diseased and then of partially restored human possibilities, is central to this work. In Querry, Greene establishes, first of all, that people in the Western world have become unhealthy.

The cause of the disease is indicated at the outset by the parody of Descartes' *cogito.* Querry is enervated, passive, and isolated because he is cut off from his circumstances. The narrative renders his gradual cure: Laughing relaxes the mind-body tension, Querry's night with Deo Gratias in the mud grants him contact with another person at an elemental level, and his recognition that he is cast about on a stream of circumstances which he cannot control puts him into a new relation with time. These events and changing attitudes are symptoms of Querry's gradual healing and the dwindling force within him of the Cartesian disease of abstraction.

The process of recovery and the image of human possibility that Querry becomes are enhanced by his association with characters who, in one way or another, are less attractive or less gifted than he is. Father Thomas, Parkinson, and Rycker exert a force on him or suggest models of human life that Querry must reject. The process of his development depends on a resistance to them and to what they represent. Rycker is a parasite who enlarges himself by draining facts of their own integrity and making them a part of his falsely expanded world; he does this because he is a lonely and insecure man who cannot admit to himself his own insignificance. Parkinson is similar to him, although Parkinson is consciously cynical and distorts his world for the sake of a reading public which needs distortions as shields against the realities of life. Parkinson acts as he does because he fears death and enjoys satisfying the public's desire for distortions. Father Thomas fears darkness and resents the anonymity thrust on him by his position as a teacher; he wants to be a martyr.

Another set of relations important to Querry's development

are those with Dr. Colin and the priests. Colin is totally involved in his circumstances by resisting them; he fights the leprosy around him, and he views himself as a part of some natural process. Querry is drawn to Colin, finding his honesty, humility, and clear-sightedness a refreshing contrast to the attitudes of others he encounters. But Colin's view of himself is more functional and specific than that to which Querry himself moves. The priests are functionaries, too, although they are oriented to more traditional myths and to vaguer ends than is Colin. This orientation of the priests makes them somewhat humorously dissociated from reality, as in the superior's mistake with the bidets. They are precious people and, in relation to the worldly Querry, almost immature. Querry, although not resisting them as he must Rycker, Parkinson, and Thomas, cannot fall in with either Colin or the priests.

A third kind of relation is with Marie. It is not so much that he derives anything from her as that she grants him occasions for development. Chief among these is the story he tells her, through which he largely clarifies the problem in his condition. The story about the boy who becomes a highly successful craftsman and lover only to find that he has become disenchanted with his life, that he has lost feeling for the king, for his work, and for women, reflects Querry's own career as an amorous, successful Catholic architect in Western Europe. What is particularly important in the story is that Querry makes clear how the boy treated the world outside of his mind, namely, as alien to him, as constituted of things to manipulate, of women to possess, and of a God to prove. As a result he cut himself off from his world, was no longer fed by it, and lost access to the nourishment his circumstances could have given to him.

Finally, Querry is helped along by his observations of the black lepers in the colony and by his association with Deo Gratias. These people are rooted in their bodies and circumstances. Their lives are primarily communal, and not individual. And they are capable of being revived by rituals, such as suggested by Deo Gratias's desire to return to a place of water to which his mother had once taken him.

In the course of his development Querry becomes a part of his world once again, although he lacks the books and pictures other people use to imitate a sense of continuity between themselves and their surroundings. He becomes a friend of Deo Gratias, a helper and companion to Marie, and an associate to Colin and the priests. In the process he becomes an "I" to himself. Through this development Querry, as the principal character, stands as a paradigm of what it is that ails Western man and how, perhaps, he can work back to a state of health.

While Greene does not complicate or enrich the image of human possibility he has given us in Querry by making him a religious man, specifically a convert to the Catholic Church, it should be remembered that the factors which most directly contribute to his restoration are constitutive of the church's life as well. The church is or should be neither individualizing nor intellectualizing in its effects on its people. Its life is rooted in mystery and communion, a life expressed in feelings and rhythms of the body. The suggestion is therefore present in the work that the recovery Querry is undergoing by laughing, being with Deo Gratias, and creating an image of himself in his confessional story to Marie is a recovery he could or should have been able to receive in the church. But Greene, quite wisely, I think, does not complicate his image of human spiritual diseases and health by bringing it into the arena of specific religious and Christian discourse. To have done so would have forced him to deal with whatever church-related ambiguities of association or opinion his readers could be counted on to have.

The principal character of Isaac Singer's *The Magician of Lublin,* Yasha Mazur, possesses at the outset of the work great confidence in his strength and ingenuity. This confidence arises from his belief that the world is open to his manipulation and understanding. It is so because God has absented himself from it; having created the world, God has now withdrawn. This leaves the world open to Yasha's use. He can perform baffling tricks, he enters intimate relationships with four women, and he fantasizes fabulous feats.

This confidence keeps Yasha from recognizing and dealing with some weaknesses which he has from the beginning. He has no real home and is alienated from his Jewish origins, he seems at times bored with his work and unstimulated by his world, he appears to need a mother and acutely feels the lack of children, and he fears death. Also, Yasha from the beginning fails to come to terms with the conflict created in him, on the one hand, by his orientation to the non-Jewish world, Warsaw and even Western Europe, and, on the other, by his deep attachment to the integrity and power of Jewish institutions and practices.

The central part of the narrative relates Yasha's increasing inability to manage his world adequately. Rather than dominate women, he is coerced by his relationships with them, particularly the Gentile, Emilia; he attempts theft and bungles the job, injuring himself in the process; he becomes increasingly bored by his world and disgusted with himself; and he feels threatened by approaching age and death. He makes promises and plans to which he has no attachment at all.

In the final part of the narrative, Yasha turns from the wreckage of his world back to his Jewish origins. Although this is difficult, given the tension he feels between the synagogue and the city, he persists, interpreting the synagogue as an occasion for discipline, order, and personal integrity. Unfortunately, his submission to law does not prevent the destruction of other people caused by his former ways, and Yasha is not spared a full recognition of his responsibility for those evils, results of the foolish goals he had been pursuing and of the utterly fantastic nature of his ambitions.

In the epilogue Yasha isolates himself from the world in a brick cell. Although his existence there is ambiguous, he experiences a measure of peace in his new situation of limitation and discipline, and he finally feels released by the world.

The difficulties that arise from Yasha's desire to manipulate the world for his own gratification are similar to those which brought Querry to the Congo in *A Burnt-Out Case*. Both characters considered the world to be open to their control, and both felt fundamentally detached from it. Although living in different centuries, countries, and religious traditions, both consider God to stand at a distance from them and their worlds. The consequences are similar, too: boredom, injury to others, and a desire to return to a simpler life. But in Singer's novel the situation is more severely depicted and the resolution of the problem more extreme. Yasha finds the alienation of himself from the world duplicated in the alienation of the religious community from the religiously distinct or secular world around it, the separation between the synagogue and the street. In addition, Singer does not allow Yasha, as Greene does Querry, to resolve the situation thousands of miles from the wreckage created by his former life. Finally, Singer does not resolve the problem by allowing Yasha to die; Yasha has to work out some modus vivendi of his own. Consequently, Singer has his character wall himself into a cell to begin a new life of separation both from Warsaw and Lublin —so severe is his understanding of the tension between the life of personal wholeness and the possibilities for human life offered by either the city or the town.

An even more severe rendering of the tension between human possibilities and external circumstances can be seen in the principal character of Flannery O'Connor's *The Violent Bear It Away*. The violent conflict between the secular world and the life of personal integrity and spiritual fullness is resolved by the principal character of this work only when he allows his demands for personal vindication and identity to die.

The tension is created in Francis Tarwater by the training he received while he lived in isolation from the rest of the world under the sole tutelage of his great uncle. When Mason dies, Francis, having been given two tasks by the old man, neglects them both and rejects the teachings of Powderhead. He does this because he succumbs to the temptation to question Mason's motives, to ridicule the origin and the assigned tasks of his supposed prophetic calling, and to desire the kind of knowledge the rest of the world can offer. As the tempter puts it, the question for Francis is not to decide between Jesus and the devil, but to decide between Jesus or himself, between "Jesus or *you*." Francis, understandably interested in self-actualization and freed by Mason's death to pursue it, decides for himself.

The second part of the narrative is dominated by the consciousness of Rayber, the uncle in the city to whom Francis turns. We learn that Rayber, while a secular, rational man, is deeply troubled. Although he has rejected the religion of Mason, the irrationality of those beliefs still attracts him. He experiences the hold religion has on him whenever he looks at anything too long or too deeply. Particularly, he experiences it when he thinks of his idiot son, Bishop. Rayber's interest in socializing Francis is an attempt, then, to repress his own religious feelings and to substitute Francis for his own son, Bishop. Rayber is a person, in other words, for whom rationality is a desperately held authority and weapon. But rationality also divorces him from his feelings and circumstances and makes him incapable of action.

Francis, in contrast, can pride himself on his ability to act, and he drowns Bishop as Rayber would not have been able to do, as also he supposedly had burned Mason's body. But by acting for Rayber, Francis maintains contact with circumstances, and circumstances will bring a character in O'Connor's fictional world to a state of emptiness. Most immediately by feeling hunger, Francis is increasingly drawn toward emptiness developed by his dealing with the world. It is in this negative way of continual privation that the call to be a prophet comes to him. In addition, the world of people around him—Rayber, Meeks, the truckdriver, and the homosexual—appears to him as violent. This violence allows the violence of Mason to appear creative, as the hunger left in him by his contacts with the rest of the world makes the food of Mason's table appear satisfying. Consequently, when Francis falls on his great uncle's grave, he views not death, but life; not emptiness, but the final feast.

In this fiction a war is going on between an autonomous human culture and the power of the irrational and transcendent. For O'Connor's fiction, the question "Jesus or *you*" is a question between Jesus and the primacy of one's consciousness, one's own understanding and will. The grotesque in her fiction is aligned with spiritual forces because it is the conscious self, the self of knowing and controlling, that must be unseated if a new, integrated person is to emerge.

In O'Connor's work the sharp contrast between a bizarre character like Mason and a caricature of the human person like Rayber is a contrast between the religious and the secular life. Rayber and the world of which he is a part is an image of human life trivialized by the authority of quantification, manipulation, and rational explanation. Mason and the world of which he is a part is an image of human life rooted in a place, celebrative toward life, and unresistive to any reality, including death. He strikes the people who know of him as insane because those spiritual values which he incarnates have been so totally forgotten, so shunted off by people, that when they are once again encountered they are alien.

In the sacramental imagery that pervades the work, baptism, Eucharist, and holy orders, O'Connor suggests that there are two kinds of violence and death in the world; the one is an end in itself, arising from the attempt to repress dimensions of life with the autonomy of individual intelligence and will, and the other leads to transformation. The violence of the kingdom leads the person through separation, hunger, and death to inclusion, fullness, and life.

III

I selected these three fictions as examples not only because in each of them character is the dominant element, and not only because in them the characters are rendered as images of human ills and possibilities, but also because these fictions represent an attack on the narrative tradition from the inside. Although the status of character has been, so to speak, undercut by an increasingly dominant atmosphere or by what has been called the "spatial" novel,[10] the image of human possibilities that the modern novel inherits from its tradition is undermined by the kind of testimony about modern human life that is figured forth in these three paradigms. In this concluding discussion I would like to suggest the investment in character that marks the modern narrative tradition and to refer to other, more theological discussions of the current image of human possibilities.

In his study of the rise and nature of modern narrative, Erich Kahler describes the process by which character comes, from the seventeenth century on, to be what I am calling paradigmatic. It does so by what he terms "ascending symbolism." The direction of this symbolism is not "from a supernatural, extra-human, or prehuman event whose reality is assumed" down to the world below, but the other way—from particulars in the natural world which are selected and enriched by the author to make them instances of "something universally human, the hu-

10. See Sharon Spencer, *Space, Time and Structure in the Modern Novel* (New York: New York University Press, 1971). Rather than speak of the spatialization of the temporal quality of narrative, I would account for the change of which she is speaking by referring to the dominance over character of atmosphere and tone.

man situation of an age or of a particular realm of living."[11] Kahler goes on to say:

> In all these great narratives a purely down-to-earth, self-contained fictional special case is so selected and so shaped, so intensified, that it becomes the essence of humanity, presenting a fundamental aspect of human life as conditioned by a given era, or the human condition of an era.[12]

Kahler's study works with the relation of modern narrative to the change of human consciousness in the postmedieval world, and character is the principal locus for observing both the symptoms of and exemplars for those changes; character in modern narrative is paradigmatic of human possibilities. Wolfgang Iser puts it this way:

> In the eighteenth century men were concerned with discovering that which the prevailing philosophy of empiricism was unable to determine: namely, what human nature consists of, how moral conduct can be developed from it, and how one can actually grasp reality itself—which, like the problem of moral conduct, had become more and more elusive in the light of the empiricists' rejection of all a priori knowledge.[13]

The primacy of individual human consciousness and the rise of the modern novel are related in such a way that character, images of individual consciousness, can generally be taken as "the central substance of fiction."[14]

As Keith Thomas in his extensive study points out,[15] it is not easy to account for the shift of authority from powers and beings other than human to individual mind and will. The shift is not due simply to a displacement of magical practices and religious beliefs by technological skills and scientific explanations; in

11. Erich Kahler, *The Inward Turn of Narrative* (Princeton: Princeton University Press, 1973), p. 57.

12. Ibid., p. 65.

13. Wolfgang Iser, *The Implied Reader* (Baltimore and London: Johns Hopkins Press, 1974), p. xiii.

14. Charles Child Walcutt, *Man's Changing Mask: Modes and Methods of Characterization in Fiction* (Minneapolis: University of Minnesota Press, 1966), p. 5.

15. Keith Thomas, *Religion and the Decline of Magic: Studies in Popular Beliefs in Sixteenth and Seventeenth Century England* (London: Weidenfeld and Nicolson, 1971), particularly pp. 641–68.

many cases the shift occurred before the technological or scientific substitutes were found. However it occurred, the change of authority marks ours from preceding eras, and it is in the context of this change that the modern novel arose. Consequently, Georg Lukács can call the novel "the epic of a world that has been abandoned by God,"[16] or has abandoned God; for the novel

> raises an individual to the infinite heights of one who must create an entire world through his experience and who must maintain that world in equilibrium—heights which no epic individual, not even Dante's, could reach, because the epic individual owed his significance to the grace accorded him, not to his pure individuality.[17]

The principal effect of modern Western fiction, then, has been to give us, as Scholes and Kellogg point out, a gallery of memorable characters.[18] These characters are paradigms of the spiritual possibilities of human life in this modern period, characters improvising worlds, like Robinson Crusoe, from themselves outward by dint of their individual, though formidable, human resources.

Because of its centrality, the "focal character of the classical novel, the conceptual Hero"[19] has very much dominated recent discussion of the state of the novel. I have already treated this phenomenon formally by relating it in the previous chapter to the rise in importance of atmosphere. Charles Walcutt makes an important point of character's reduction by the emphasis on a more distant perspective or point of view, a distance which tends to rob character of the depth and complexity it once had.[20] And in her study of the spatial novel, Sharon Spencer cites as peculiarly a matter of this century that writers are interested primarily in creating not characters, but realms.

16. Georg Lukács, *The Theory of the Novel: A Historico-philosophical Essay on the Forms of Great Epic Literature*, trans. Anna Bostock (Cambridge: M.I.T. Press, 1971), p. 88. See also, pp. 90–93.
17. Ibid., p. 83.
18. Scholes and Kellogg, *Nature of Narrative*, p. 192.
19. Sean O'Faolain, *The Vanishing Hero: Studies in the Novelists of the Twenties* (London: Eyre and Spottiswoode, 1956), p. 14.
20. See Walcutt, *Man's Changing Mask*.

The creator of a world will want to put in people, but much more besides: streets; buildings; parks; stores; cars; animals; systems of thought; replicas of art works; religious attitudes; theories of economics, government, psychology; and so on. The character becomes, then, but one of many elements of the total world.[21]

In fictions of this kind, not unlike those used as examples in chapter 1, character becomes at most "a medium for the expression of some particularized view of the reality constructed in the book in which he appears."[22] Formally, this change in emphasis can be described as a growing dominance of other narrative elements, particularly of atmosphere and tone, although Professor Spencer wants to posit a far more radical break of spatial fiction from the tradition than my formulation of the matter would suggest.

What is at stake in these discussions of the novel is the status of character in a time in which the sufficiency and autonomy of individual human consciousness has become at some points a matter of doubt and anxiety. In a recent book, John Vernon makes this situation very clear.[23] He deals with a central ingredient of the intellectual background of the modern novel, namely, the proclivity of the Western mind to abstract itself from its context and to treat its world as though it were only spatial, free from time. The spatialization of time is not, as with Spencer, then, a peculiarly recent phenomenon; Vernon would relate it to realism generally, the tendency to turn the world into a map, to freeze time, and to place perspective (as manipulation) in control. Vernon feels that this epistemological stance, found in and supported by the modern novel, has resulted in the trivialization and reduction of human life and that it is now in the process of being overthrown. What will arise in its place are paradigms of human life emphasizing continuity and relationship with circumstances, particularly temporality.

The three novels examined above give testimony to Vernon's argument. The creators of the three principal characters seem

21. Spencer, *Space, Time and Structure in the Modern Novel*, p. 2.
22. Ibid., p. 5.
23. John Vernon, *The Garden and the Map: Schizophrenia in Twentieth Century Literature and Culture* (Urbana: University of Illinois Press, 1973).

well aware of the spiritual problems that result from the alienation of individual consciousness from its circumstances and its
assumption of primacy and autonomy. Querry comes to Africa
as a man totally depleted by his disconnection from his surroundings, and he is restored in the Congo when the strain of
separation from context, particularly from his body, is relaxed.
Yasha Mazur, an enlightened Jew, excuses God from his world
in order to exert his own mastery over it, but the results of this
self-evaluation are disastrous. While Francis Tarwater finds
nothing in the city to feed him, he is reborn to new possibilities
when he quits his attempts to make and maintain a world of
his own.

Although these characters are exhausted, foolish, or insignifi-
cant men, they are, by the process of what Kahler calls "ascending symbolism," no less paradigmatic for their ordinariness,
for they are made by their creators into images of human limitations and potential conditioned by the modern era. They have
power, as do all characters in fiction, because they are paradigms, in this instance paradigms of the victimization of human
potential by the heritage of abstracted consciousness and of the
recovery of lost personal potential through a radical alteration of
orientation.

Although character is organically related to the other elements and shaped by and for them as well, character in itself is
an image of human possibilities rendered by the author, as, so to
speak, standing on its own feet, and it may be possible to say
that the tradition has been dominated by the attempt to emphasize this potential in narrative; further, this inherited emphasis,
with its epistemological and spiritual underpinnings and consequences, is now in the process, in several ways, of being altered.
Although it is conditioned by atmosphere, changed by plot, and
subjected to the element of perspective in tone, character by
itself is still an objective image of the human as such. When
character becomes dominant in a fiction, relatively free from
atmosphere, plot, and tone, it increasingly becomes paradigmatic
of the problems and potentials within human life.

A second answer, then, to the question, Why can narratives
have religious meaning? is that character is an image of human
possibilities, a paradigm of what man is, can be, should be, or
must be. As such, it plays a role analogous to the heroes, saints,

and deified beings who are images of human possibilities in stories within religious communities. This does not mean that characters in fiction are religious figures of that kind. But as paradigms they are easily enriched and complicated with religious associations and can even become transfigurations of religious figures like Jesus,[24] Buddha,[25] or Prometheus.[26] Also, they are directly relevant to religious discussions that arise from reflection on religiously authoritative figures and exemplars.

Of course, a religious person, working as Kahler describes him with figures related to some extrahuman or prehuman source, will always be at some distance, when he speaks of human possibilities, from discussions about human potential derived from characters who are, to use Kahler's phrase again, "ascending symbols." But the area between the two is traversed by novelists who enlarge on these possibilities religiously and theologically, as in the instances we have seen, and by theologians who are willing to talk in the marketplace about religion as a means of actualizing human possibilities. Such functional views of religion tend to shape current religious discussion, and one finds in thinkers such as Harvey Cox, Sam Keen, Robert Bellah, Langdon Gilkey, and Herbert Richardson an advocacy of religion as a way of opening up possibilities of human self-actualization.

In these discussions, religion is called on to perform at least three functions. The first of these is to provide a "supreme fiction" by which a fragmented world can be thought of as unified. Wallace Stevens is fairly important to such discussions since he, as J. Hillis Miller puts it, felt the threat of a fragmented world: "subject, object, words, other minds, the supernatural—each of these realms is divorced from the others, and man finds himself one of the 'poor fragments of a broken world.' "[27] Religion can be used, according to such discussions, to grant an individual

---

24. See Theodore Ziolkowski, *Fictional Transfigurations of Jesus* (Princeton: Princeton University Press, 1972).

25. See Hermann Hesse, *Siddhartha*, trans. Hilda Rosner (New York: New Directions, 1951).

26. See William F. Lynch, *Christ and Prometheus: A New Image of the Secular* (Notre Dame, Indiana: University of Notre Dame Press, 1970).

27. J. Hillis Miller, *Poets of Reality: Six Twentieth-Century Writers* (Cambridge: Harvard University Press, 1965), p. 2.

relief from the problem of fragmentation by providing at least a semblance of unity. Secondly, religion can deliver a person from unnecessarily restricting and confining expectations. A person need not be cabined by the feasible, the predictable, by continuity with what has already been accomplished; he can look for the unexpected, can cultivate the gratuitous, and religion can stimulate an interest in doing that, can enlarge a person's conception of possibilities. Finally, these discussants, particularly people like Sam Keen, Richard Rubenstein, and David Miller,[28] direct attention not toward a religious orientation to a sky god and to laws, but to the earth, the unconscious, and spontaneity. We are now at the verge of witnessing a new development of reverence for and an interest in the mother deities and chthonic gods, a development anticipated in literature by artists, including such writers as D. H. Lawrence, William Faulkner, Herman Hesse, Robert Graves, Aldous Huxley, Lawrence Durrell, and Henry Miller.

This functional view of religion as a means to enhance and expand the image of man in recent marketplace discussions will not do for a religious man, of course. Given to him in his sacred stories are images of evil and good, destruction and creativity, stasis and transformation, and these are paradigmatic, directly or indirectly, of human possibilities. However, in the situation of separation between the characters of modern narrative and the paradigmatic figures of sacred stories, novels of the kind we have suggested and religious discussions to which brief reference has been made serve well the need for some exploration of a middle ground between the two. More important for this study, the novels and religious discussions reveal how and why character in modern narrative naturally draws to itself complications and enrichments of a religious nature; they do so because character gathers status as a paradigm of human possibility and is analogous to the importance of spiritually authoritative figures in religious life.

28. See Sam Keen, *To a Dancing God* (New York: Harper & Row, 1970); Richard Rubenstein, *After Auschwitz: Radical Theology and Contemporary Judaism* (Indianapolis: Bobbs-Merrill Co., 1966); and David L. Miller, *The New Polytheism: Rebirth of the Gods and Goddesses* (New York: Harper & Row, 1974).

3

Plot and Process

I

From among the several problems within the topic of plot in modern narrative this chapter will give most direct attention to the question of whether plots can still be mimetic. Can a plot, since it gives some order or shape to the time of a narrative, reflect time as we experience it? Or is time as we experience it so broken, incoherent, or meaningless that plots turn narrative time into something very different from our other senses of time? In other words, are plots wholly determined by "plotting"?

There is little question that time is a major preoccupation of Western thought and that it has become a serious problem in our own day. We live now in what Mircea Eliade refers to as the "terror of history."[1] He sees this experience of time as the consequence of several developments. First, history gradually became dissociated from those natural cycles of human time which, because they were repeated and rehearsed in myths and rituals, returned a people to their origins. This dissociation took place when heroes and ancestors were believed to have accomplished deeds which, for good or evil, were irreversible, and separated time from the eternal round and from fresh beginnings. Second, Biblical religion and, therefore, Judaism and Christianity, accomplished a separation of history from nature and a locating of divine revelation primarily in history, a locus least susceptible, for Eliade, to hierophany. A number of developments resulted, including the imputation of novelty and irreversibility to all actions, the temporal definition of man, the dis-

1. Mircea Eliade, *Cosmos and History: The Myth of the Eternal Return,* trans. Willard R. Trask, Harper Torchbooks (New York: Harper & Row, 1959), chap. 4.

sociation of time from nature, and the subordination of the meaning of events to the fact of their having happened.[2] Eliade contends that the rationalistic interpretations of history and "historicism" could not have developed in the last century without lingering, religious-like beliefs and that the terror of history results from an erosion of those vulnerable remainders of a previous, more religious period. Now, Eliade concludes, Western man has neither defenses against, nor recourses from, the terror of history.

Aggravating the situation to which Eliade is referring, of course, is the modern separation of public or external from private or internal time. Due to the need for order created by larger urban settings and developing mass transportation, impersonal time, a time with which a person himself would have very ambiguous relations, increased in use and exactitude.[3] Problems of this kind—the question of the meaning or coherence of history and the question of the relation of clock time to personal time—are examples of the ways in which time is a matter of major modern uncertainty and in which that uncertainty creates an unsettled context for discussing the force and meaning of plots in modern narratives.

In addition to this set of problems there are equally difficult formal matters. The first of these I have already indicated, namely, the spatialization of narrative.[4] Although I disagree with attempts to construe this characteristic of modern narrative as a radical break with the tradition, and although I account for it by discussing the domination of time in modern narrative by the elements of atmosphere and tone, there is no doubt about

2. Important in this development, too, is the notion arising in the Renaissance that things have a history. See, e.g., George Kubler, *The Shape of Time* (New Haven: Yale University Press, 1962).
3. See Hans Meyerhoff, *Time in Literature* (Berkeley and Los Angeles: University of California Press, 1955), Theodore Ziolkowski. "The Discordant Clocks" in his *Dimensions of the Modern Novel: German Texts and European Contexts* (Princeton: Princeton University Press, 1969), and Nathan A. Scott, Jr., "Mimesis and Time in Modern Literature" in his *The Broken Center: Studies in the Theological Horizon of Modern Literature* (New Haven and London: Yale University Press, 1966), pp. 28–76.
4. See, e.g., Sharon Spencer, *Space, Time and Structure in the Modern Novel* (New York: New York University Press, 1971) and Cary Nelson, *The Incarnate Word: Literature as Verbal Space* (Urbana, Chicago, and London: University of Illinois Press, 1973).

the ambiguous position into which plot is put when mobile-like structures such as in *The Sybil,* urban settings such as in *The Clown,* and the emphasis on perspectives such as in *The Plague,* juxtapose times, dissolve time, or cut time up into views of it. An equally important problem has been carefully exposed recently by Meir Sternberg.[5] He points out the critical confusion created by theorists of plot in fiction when they fail to distinguish between what he refers to as the *fabula* and the *sujet.* The *fabula* refers, to put it simply, to the chronology or even the causal sequence of events as they can be thought to have occurred, and the *sujet* refers to the way in which those events are presented in the narrative: scrambled, interrupted, selected, and interpreted by one perspective or many perspectives. Without minimizing the importance of Professor Sternberg's point, however, I would suggest that he is talking about the subjection of plot to tone. That is, one way in which the modern novel has handled contemporary confusion about time has been to subject time either to atmosphere or to tone. And rather than to posit a *fabula* in which the sequence of events is made clear, helpful as that exercise may be, it may be better to account for the ways in which plot is modified and reduced in a particular fiction under the pressure of other elements.

It is important for the life of the form, I think, to resist the idea that because time is generally a problem, plot can no longer be a dominant element in a fiction; there are no convincing reasons why plot is no longer potentially a principal power and meaning source for a narrative. Charles Walcutt reminds us:

> if we recall that Aristotle said a tragedy could be represented without character, whereas the modern world thinks that character is the source from which action flows, we see that there can be a vast difference in the relative importance of these two elements.[6]

So also, we could go on to say, we can judge our own distance from our immediate past by the diminution of both character

5. Meir Sternberg, "What is Exposition? An Essay in Temporal Delimitation," in *The Theory of the Novel: New Essays,* ed. John Halperin (New York: Oxford University Press, 1974), pp. 25–70.

6. Charles Child Walcutt, *Man's Changing Mask: Modes and Methods of Characterization in Fiction* (Minneapolis: University of Minnesota Press, 1966), p. 16.

and plot at the hands of atmosphere and tone. But these changes of emphasis do not utterly destroy the possibilities within character and plot as they also do not solve the problems associated with them. The implied artist can even now allow plot to dominate his fictional world, thereby granting the flow or the pattern of circumstances and events primary status, rather than the limiting or enabling conditions of the fictional world, the achievements or failures of human understanding and control, or the choices, articulations, and perspectives of his image of personal presence.

When most effective, plot draws little attention to itself; it seems unforced by tone, unplotted, natural. When this occurs, plot is not so much an image of time collected as it is an image of time as a process, whether for good or evil, whether creative or destructive, meaningful or not. Plots are images of recognizable processes, particularly of growth or dissolution. Although it may be often overshadowed by other elements, plot as an image of process can still control a fiction; when it does, the linear, temporal quality of the form has been developed into a coherent process.

The question, now, is whether or not plot, when it becomes an image of coherent and even natural process, distances a fiction from life. If, as we have suggested, the meaningfulness of time as experienced is open to question, or even generally denied, narratives cannot lightly exert their most formal characteristic, namely, their structuring of time, even if that structuring is nothing more than what can be suggested by beginning and ending. Even if a fiction does nothing as assertive as suggested by this statement—"The conventional plot assumes that life is not meaningless, that the universe is essentially rational and causal"[7]—plot in fiction does stake out a portion of time, isolating it to a degree, and, consequently perhaps, dissociating it radically from our everyday experience of time. The question, in a word, then, is whether time in fiction thereby becomes not so much artful as artificial.

The problem of plot's relation to time as we experience it outside of works of fiction is at the center of Frank Kermode's important study, *The Sense of an Ending.* He makes clear the

7. Richard F. Dietrich and Roger H. Sundell, *The Art of Fiction* (New York: Holt, Rinehart and Winston, 1967), p. 48.

fact that the status of plot in the contemporary literary field has been called seriously into question because of the loss in our society of any sense that our shared time is actually a plot, divinely guided from beginning to ending. The substitution of fiction for myth is, for Kermode, the replacement of some identity between time and its meaning with conscious fabrication of the illusion. Events have no meaning, however much people mistakenly think that they do. Even today, when our contemporaries lend significance to our time by thinking of it as actually transitional, unprecedented, or fraught with crisis, they are victims of myth-making habits.[8]

His dissociation of meaning from time allows Kermode to place a very high value on fictional plots, however artificial they may be. For plots arise from the need to humanize time by turning merely sequential time into a concord, into a time oriented to a beginning, and, particularly, to an ending. Kermode believes the need for an ending is deeply embedded in the human imagination and makes itself felt despite repeated experiences of time as different from what our need for endings interprets time to be. The thirst for temporal concords also accounts, according to his thesis, for the writing and the reading of fictions.

To illustrate the process of humanizing time by making concords of it, Kermode refers to the *tick* and *tock* of a clock. Experiments reveal, he claims, that people who listen to these sounds can render accurately the interval between *tick* and *tock* after the clock has been removed, but they have no reliable recall of the interval between *tock* and *tick*. He concludes, then:

> The clock's *tick-tock* I take to be a model of what we call a plot, an organization that humanizes time by giving it form; and the interval between *tock* and *tick* represents purely successive, disorganized time of the sort we need to humanize.[9]

Fictions arise out of the action of the imagination upon time, out of the imaginative act of unifying chaotic time, turning it into a concord. He describes this act at one point by using sexual imagery: "Contingency is nauseous and viscous; it has been

8. Frank Kermode, *The Sense of an Ending* (New York: Oxford University Press, 1967), p. 101.
9. Ibid., p. 45.

suggested that the figure is ultimately sexual. This is unformed matter, *materia, matrix;* Roquentin's is ultimately the form-giving male role."[10] The writing of fiction arises out of a fear of or resistance to chaos, and fictional time resembles the time of the angels, something other than the time in which we mortals ordinarily live.

Kermode separates time as we experience it, time as it is, from time as we would like or imagine it to be; he separates fictional time from real time. Plots, then, are not mimetic. In fact, there are no plots in fiction; there is only plotting, the imposition of order, beginning and ending, on time. The question then becomes, to repeat it, whether plots can be delivered from plotting, whether they can be reflective or imitative of time as we experience it.

The possibility which Kermode did not pursue is to suggest that plots in fiction, while dissociated from sequential or linear time, may remind us, to return to our opening discussion of Eliade, of traditional or repeatable time. Some literary theorists do pursue this possibility and thereby indicate that plots are unlike merely sequential time because they are more like cyclical time, because they imitate recurring processes. Such theorists, of course, are generally referred to as myth critics. Although it had its origins in a reaction to New Criticism, as John Vickery reminds us,[11] myth criticism constitutes as much a way of going beyond Kermode as it does a way of compensating for formalism, since both Kermode and New Criticism cut fictions off from a relationship with time and our wider experience of it. We see how this would be the case in the thought of Ernst Cassirer for whom it is characteristic of the mythic or nonscientific mind to be in close relation to the world. Scientific thinking expunges the subjective in its claims for objectivity while mythical thinking knows no gap between what is seen and what it means for the beholder. As he says, "Whereas scientific thought takes an attitude of inquiry and doubt toward the 'object' with its claim of objectivity and necessity, myth knows no such opposition.

10. Ibid., p. 136.

11. John B. Vickery, ed., *Myth and Literature: Contemporary Theory and Practice* (Lincoln: University of Nebraska Press, 1966), p. x.

It 'has' the object only insofar as it is overpowered by it."[12] Art is expressive for Cassirer of this kind of more basic, integrated human relation to the world and not, as is fiction for Kermode, the imposition of alien forms on it.

Another theorist who has influenced myth critics deeply is Carl Jung. In his essay on "Psychology and Literature," Jung relates the writing of fiction to the contact with more primary and often excluded elements of a person's life, particularly the unconscious. Art compensates for the day-light world to which he believes moderns have given ascendency; art allows the imagination to give us images of the collective unconscious. The artist, then, far from imposing something of his own making on time, gives us images of "collective man," of those structures and figures which, without our realizing it, underlie our daily, day-light attitudes and acts. Jung says:

> The creative process has feminine quality, and the creative work arises from the unconscious depths—we might say, from the realm of the mothers. Whenever the creative force predominates, human life is ruled and moulded by the unconscious as against the active will, and the conscious ego is swept along on a subterranean current, being nothing more than a helpless observer of events.[13]

Rather than imposing or constructing plots, then, the imagination allows plots to be reflective or expressive of images, processes, and forces which are at work in the unconscious.

Whether because they arise from a basic intellectual or psychic activity or, as with Malinowski and Durkheim, they engage the reader in processes by which the norms of a culture are tested or affirmed, plots are not so much imposed as they are evoked, and the time which they reflect is not so much linear as it is repetitious and, to use Eliade's word, traditional. As Philip Rahv puts it:

> One essential function of myth shared by all writers is that in merging past and present it releases us from the flux of tem-

---

12. Ernst Cassirer, *The Philosophy of Symbolic Forms*, vol. 2, *Mythical Thought*, trans. Ralph Manheim (New Haven: Yale University Press, 1955), p. 74.
13. Carl Jung, *Modern Man In Search of a Soul* (New York: Harcourt, Brace & Co., 1934), p. 170.

porality, arresting change in the timeless, the permanent, the ever-recurrent conceived as "sacred repetition."[14]

It is this quality that allows the reader to resonate, according to Norman Holland, to reexperience "that earlier sense of being merged into a larger matrix, a living forever in a role laid down from time immemorial."[15]

> In "taking in" a poem, story, or drama, we partly regress to that state where we did not differentiate what happened "in here" from what went on "out there." Our conscious knowledge of a timeless, mythic substructure furthers this original "as if."[16]

The time of literature overcomes the split between consciously ordered and merely sequential time that Kermode establishes, and it does this by viewing the order and significance of time as coincident with our sense of it.

Myth critics such as Philip Wheelwright and Joseph Campbell draw our attention even more directly to plot when they view the time of a narrative as imitative of processes within the development of the self. Wheelwright says, for example:

> Every change of human condition—birth, puberty, initiation, betrothal, marriage, pregnancy, paternity, specialization of occupation, death—is mythopoetically regarded as a passage from a state of self that is dying to a state of self newly born. Such events do not merely happen to an individual on the outside, they change the very thing he *is*. . . .[17]

In his *The Hero With a Thousand Faces,* Joseph Campbell says that "the purpose and actual effect of these [primitive rituals] was to conduct people across those difficult thresholds of transformation that demand a change in the patterns not only of conscious but also of unconscious life."[18] Similarly, Herbert Weisinger refers to the protagonist's passage from ignorance to wisdom, to Aristotle's recognition, as epitomizing the kind of

14. Philip Rahv, "The Myth and the Powerhouse," in Vickery, *Myth and Literature*, p. 111.
15. Norman Holland, *The Dynamics of Literary Response* (New York: Oxford University Press, 1968), p. 248.
16. Ibid., p. 260.
17. Philip Wheelwright, "Notes on Mythopoeia," in Vickery, *Myth and Literature*, pp. 64–65.
18. Joseph Campbell, *The Hero With a Thousand Faces* (Cleveland and New York: World Publishing Co., 1956), p. 10.

process of rebirth that it is the effect of literary plots to imitate or create.[19] And in *The American Adam,* R. W. B. Lewis calls attention to the process of initiation, the move from innocence to experience; he thinks that the effect of American narrative, particularly in the nineteenth century, is to reflect the passage from some point prior to life to full engagement with it.

Although it may be intended as only a heuristic device, Northrop Frye's theory of plots ought finally to be mentioned as suggestive of the relation of plot to kinds of processes, for Frye places the plots of literature over a grid of seasonal cycles. The mythos of spring is related to comic plots, particularly the integration of character into society or nature. The mythos of summer is related to romance, the dreamlike and often quite static situation of a stable and humanly supportive society. The mythos of autumn suggests tragic plots, decay of society and an individual's relation to it. Finally, the mythos of winter suggests ironic literature, plots of alienation and of a fallen or objectionable society. These plots shade off into one another, so that, for example, the winter mythos is related to spring as new possibilities arise in a plot due to the superior moral position of the principal character as a victim of an evil society.[20]

All of these theorists see the time of a narrative as at least potentially reflective or imitative of the time of human experience generally, and the effect of their work is to relate the time of plots to recurring psychic, social, or natural processes. Tacit agreement, secondly, can be detected among them in that they view plots as repetitive and tend, thereby, to dissociate meaningful plot from linear time, from history.

Of course, myth critics can, in their reaction to formalism, fall under the possible new critical judgment of the heresy of paraphrase.[21] Even more importantly, myth critics may have an a priori interest in something psychic, social, or religious that underlies their interest in narrative time, and they can use litera-

19. Herbert Weisinger, "The Myth and Ritual Approach to Shakespearean Tragedy," in Vickery, *Myth and Literature,* p. 151.
20. Northrop Frye, *Anatomy of Criticism* (New York: Atheneum, 1966), pp. 163-239.
21. See Wallace W. Douglas, "The Meaning of 'Myth' in Modern Criticism," *Modern Philology* (May, 1953): 232-42.

ture in an apologetics for their interests.[22] Or they may possibly view literature as a window through which something more important than the literary work can be seen. If this kind of reductionism or dogmatism is to be avoided, the relations drawn between literary plots and life processes must be drawn in such a way that it is the plot that suggests the process and not the process which determines the plot. In addition, myth critics can be charged with a nostalgia for a former age, as Herbert Weisinger points out; there can be implied a distrust or even rejection of the time in which we now live, even a distrust of intellect and science in favor of something from a previous age or of emotion or of intellectual immaturity. Surely, no theory of literature can exist by virtue of hostility to our own time or to some other aspect of human endeavor. But we also need not equate intellectual maturity and enfranchisement in our own historical period with full and unquestioning acceptance of the Sartrean epistemology which Kermode presupposes. We need an epistemology which will allow us to see the continuity, or at least the contiguity, of kinds of knowledge, scientific and other, with one another, and one which will allow us to see the relation of thinking to kinds of "knowledge" which arise from our basic, prereflective participation in our circumstances, including, of course, time. Although it may be open to misuse, myth criticism strikes me as a contribution to the present need of rescuing plot from the kind of isolation in which Kermode places it, of seeing plot as related to experienced time. The way in which these theorists do that is to see literary plots as reflective of kinds of psychic, social, and natural processes. To return to Eliade, they have made the time of narrative meaningful by delivering it from the terrors of history and associating it with time as cyclical, repetitive, and tied to natural processes—a situation roughly parallel to time as Eliade sees it in traditional societies.

Despite the strain placed on plot by forces within the form, primarily atmosphere and tone, and despite the problem that time has become for us in this century, plot need not be intimidated or uniquely isolated from daily life. Plot, as a reflection of kinds of human processes, moreover, can easily draw to itself associations and enrichments suggestive, as we shall see, of religious rituals. But before continuing this discussion, we should

22. Holland, *Dynamics of Literary Response*, pp. 243-61.

look at three works of fiction in which plot is dominant, in which plot reflects a process, and in which the process is complicated by association with religious ritual. Then we shall be in a position once again to take up the question of time in modern narrative and its relation to the terror of history.

II

To say that plot is the dominant element of William Golding's *The Spire* is to make the judgment that the process of building the tower and spire for the cathedral, a process in which the dean figures prominently, is not something that can be wholly accounted for by references to his will, important as his own will may be. For as Jocelin victimizes the builders and other people under his charge for the project's sake, it can also be said that Jocelin is himself taken in and taken along by events over which he has but partial control.

The three parts of the plot, each part rendered in four chapters, correspond to the stages of construction. The first, covering roughly a year of time, describes the circumstances surrounding the project, the basis for building the spire, and some of the consequences of its erection. The second part, chapters five through eight, gives us events of the second year, primarily the practical completion of the tower and spire. In the third part, the struggle to erect the spire is ended, and the consequences of the project, particularly for Jocelin, are rendered, including his perception of what the cost for the spire has been to him and to the church, as well as the reversal of his fortune, the loss of his position, and his death.

Building the spire is something Jocelin feels he must do, since the project satisfies his uncertainty as to why, at a young age and quite gratuitously, he was cast into his office as dean of the cathedral. He believes, quite understandably, that this unusual event must have some reason or purpose, and he takes that purpose to lie in some particular task; casting about, possibly, for a special work, he, not surprisingly, concludes that supplying the missing spire would fill the bill. In addition, he believes that this conclusion was confirmed by a vision.

In this part it also becomes clear that the decision to build the spire is one made as much for Jocelin as by him because of his obviously neurotic sexual feelings. He has a need to compensate for his sexual frustrations or, for whatever the many reasons may be, to display his manliness. The building of the spire all along is related to Jocelin's need for sexual gratification.

The religious and psychological forces coercing his decision are placed in tension with the facts. Jocelin must sacrifice other things to the project. Money for the construction comes from his aunt as a bribe to grant her burial in the church. Timber comes from a man who wants, in exchange, the ordination of his son, Ivo, as canon, despite the boy's lack of qualifications for or interest in the position. Furthermore, Jocelin must subvert his relation to the church and individuals in order to carry on the project. He virtually imprisons the master builder, Roger, and exploits the unfortunate relationship between the impotent Pangall and his wife, Goody, by allowing the attraction between Goody and Roger to develop. In general, the church's rituals are almost brought to a halt, as Jocelin places all of his energy into the two-year project of building the spire. Finally, the physical conditions are unfit for the spire; the builders fail to find solid ground under the building to support the weight.

In the second part the tensions suggested in the first become severe. For Jocelin it is a matter not only of increasing the sense of risk, but also of increasing his faith. As the construction continues, he begins to realize what is involved, the cost and the danger. He discovers that Roger has no precedent to follow and that he has to calculate the spire into being as he goes along, weighing strength against mass. He learns that Roger fears heights. And, by seeing his own reflection, he recognizes what the cost of the project has been to himself.

Added to the tension between risk or cost and faith stands the relation of joy to guilt. The higher the spire rises, the happier Jocelin becomes, like a boy in a high tree. But the height also creates guilt and anxiety. The workmen defect, Roger drinks more heavily, and Jocelin recognizes what he is doing to other people and to the church.

A symbolic center is formed in this second part by Goody's delivery and death. As the Church of Our Lady is filled with unclean workmen and violated by this project, the supposedly virgin Goody dies in childbirth. But this element also continues to stimulate Jocelin's interest in the project; as he had been all along sexually attracted to Goody and, perhaps, had even arranged her marriage to Pangall so that no other man would have her, now he is attracted to her as the ascended goal toward whom the erection can be directed.

The third part renders the experiences of recognition and reversal that come to Jocelin as a result of this project. He learns, first of all, the crucial truth of his appointment to office, namely, that it was not a special divine act, but the result of a postcoital whim of his aunt's royal lover. He also is judged in this part for having neglected the real work of the church, its rhythms of praise. His fortune is reversed as well; he loses his position and dies.

On the other hand, the recognition and reversal do not cancel the worth of the project. For one thing, Jocelin becomes a more impressive person at the end; he hammers in the relic nail and visits Roger to ask forgiveness. But more than that, the spire itself, for all its cost and despite the risks, stands. It is, even with its cost, a magnificent achievement which has already caused a reorientation of the human life around it.

The plot of this work, then, is a process by which a number of matters concerning human activity are revealed. First, creative acts and achievements, while splendid when considered in isolation from the context in which they arose, can be seen, on closer scrutiny, to arise also from neurotic impulses and to be very costly to circumstances and to other people. At one level the plot reveals that something so noble as a cathedral spire is not exempt from the taint of its origins in human emotional disturbance nor from the moral ambiguities of its heavy cost in human energy and life. Second, the plot reveals that creative acts and achievements are rooted in human pride, in the identification of desire with circumstances, of ego with world. By building higher than anyone, Jocelin has over-stepped a boundary, and the results of such prideful risk-taking, while in this case not the collapse of the entire project, are fully faced. Jocelin hurts himself, others, and the church; the judgment upon him, on his mistakes, negligence, and pride, are justified. But however much it may be said that there are meanings of this kind revealed by the plot, it can also be said that a third matter is more important, namely, that, even though people may be limited by their experience and knowledge, they are able to move beyond these limitations to new achievements. Jocelin, although neurotic, proud, and ignorant of what he could not have known, particularly the details of his appointment to office, creates something new. The plot celebrates, in other words, the human capacity to go beyond the limits of experience and ignorance in creative acts. The creative power of man, despite his sickness, pride, and ignorance, results in this splendid thing, the spire, with its own tremendous justification for being there.

By placing his narrative in the late Middle Ages and by suggesting analogues between his story and other great plots in the heritage of Western thought—the eating of the fruit in Eden, the building of the tower of Babel and the ark of Noah, and the story of Prometheus' defiance of Zeus—Golding has suggested an Aristotelian universality in the historical event of Salisbury's spire which his novel reconstructs. Both because of its humanistically celebrative plot and because of the universal implications of that plot, it is a work reminiscent of the kind of tragedy Sophocles imagined and the kind which Aristotle so much admired.

For our purposes, however, it is important to point out what Golding has suggested about kinds of time in this plot-dominated fiction. The linear time created by the protracted project and the effort to erect a new thing stands in a contradictory relation to the time celebrated by the church—its "fabric of praise," its rituals, repetitions, and return to original time. But this linear time is not, thereby, without meaning. It is itself a process which has, at least, analogues in other creative acts. Through its plot, Golding's novel reflects or reveals something in our world, namely, that history is not merely a matter of human intentions and acts but is constituted, too, of processes, although unrepeated, in which a person, willy-nilly, finds himself caught whenever he acts—processes, indeed, which largely account for his actions in the first place. Furthermore, to say this is not to diminish human life at all, but rather to account at least in part for the fact that human life is capable of new and startling things. No evolutionary theory of human or social development is here implied. Rather, and more simply, it is suggested that human actions arise out of and set loose, for good as well as ill, processes which make them more far-reaching than a person can possibly be aware of. And to look at history in terms of human actions or achievements only is to look merely at occasions, symptoms, and results.

Although plot is also the dominant element of Nathanael West's *Miss Lonelyhearts,* its meaning is quite different from that of *The Spire.* The process by which the principal character's life is complicated and destroyed takes on, through images connected with sacrificial rituals, the suggestion that he dies as a victim.

The plot's first part, in which the gravely problematic situation is revealed, moves from the beginning to the moment when Miss Lonelyhearts leaves Betty's apartment. The situation is problematic because Miss Lonelyhearts finds that his new responsibilities as a writer of the newspaper's advice column subject him to great pressure. Shrike, the feature editor, makes this clear by indicating and then mocking the quasi-priestly position in which those who read and write to Miss Lonelyhearts place this person. In addition, Miss Lonelyhearts discovers that people writing to the column request advice on specific courses of action, and Miss Lonelyhearts, as a newspaper writer and son of a Baptist minister, is accustomed neither to the kinds of problems put before him by the letters nor to the call for specific actions to alleviate them. The position and his background call for words, and these seem to him increasingly dissociated from the circumstances in which his readers are trying to carry forward their lives.

An insight into his formerly more limited world is granted the reader by Miss Lonelyhearts's association with Betty, who continues, as Miss Lonelyhearts no longer can, to avoid problems simply by excluding them from her attention. Her world is clean and neat, sharply delimited. But in her apartment he finds himself annoyed by her innocence, and he acts rudely toward her.

At about this time Miss Lonelyhearts is also having dreams of a compensating and projecting nature. In one he plays the role of a magician, able to work his world to his own and the audience's satisfaction. In another, the sacrifice of a lamb is enacted. Images from these dreams, with the liturgical material satirically provided by Shrike and such things as the crucifix hanging in his room, serve to enrich and complicate the meaning of the plot with suggestions of its ritualistic nature.

In the second part, from the falling out with Betty to their vacation in the country and return, the problematic situation becomes more complicated the more Miss Lonelyhearts tries to do something about it. At one point he becomes sufficiently frustrated by the problem, or angered by the threat to his sense of adequacy posed by insoluble problems, that he becomes violent, twisting the old man's arm. Next he tries forms of escape— sleep, whisky, and sex—although these merely postpone facing the situation. He turns, also, to his major resource, words and ideas, but his attempts to produce adequate replies produce only trite homilies on optimism that fall like tired clichés. He undergoes the chastisement that sadistic Shrike provides, tormenting him with a list of the world's best solutions to human limitation and misery. His most significant act in this part is to become involved with the writer of one of the many letters, but his visit to Mrs. Doyle reveals that there is nothing he can do for her. In fact, contact with her threatens to drag him down into the sealike chaos of her many woes. Having tried almost everything, he runs off to the country with Betty for a few days of innocence and peace.

In the last part, from the return to the city until the end, Miss Lonelyhearts attempts a final solution to the problem; he decides that what is needed as a response to the situation is not so much that he do something as that he become some kind of person adequate to the situation. First of all, he must become humble. In this achieved state of alienation from confidence in his own resources, he feels a new strength and solidity developing within him; indeed, he feels Christ-like. But his acts are no more successful than before. He fails completely in his attempts with the Doyles, and when he feels called by the doorbell to a Christ-like act, he is accidentally shot and falls down the stairway to his own apparently meaningless death.

The plot moves from the violent situation created for Miss Lonelyhearts when he finds himself having to respond to insoluble problems, through attempts at adequate responses which only postpone, prolong, or aggravate the already problematic situation, to his well-intended but catastrophic and inconsequential act at the end. Given the position of having to give solutions to insoluble problems, Miss Lonelyhearts can either admit to his own inadequacy and adjust his self-identity accordingly or he can be consumed in the attempt to provide an adequate response. Trying to match himself and his situation, he is destroyed.

As I have already noted, the meaning of the plot is complicated and enriched by images connected with rituals and by conversations and thoughts concerning religious models, beliefs, and actions. This complication may mean either of two things: It may mean that since Miss Lonelyhearts was unsuccessful in his attempts to respond adequately to a problematic world, the religious complications provided are likewise revealed to be inadequate, thereby suggesting that a religious solution to insoluble problems is no more effective than is Miss Lonelyhearts's; or it may mean that, although he was unsuccessful in handling adequately the problems he encountered, he gave meaning to his life and bore witness to that meaning by becoming himself a sacrificial victim to a troubled world.

While there may be other valid interpretations of the plot, and while I tend to favor the second of the above two, discussion of the meaning of the plot should not obscure the principal point with which we are dealing, namely, that plot can dominate a work, can be mimetic of kinds of processes within our world. In this case, the story illustrates what happens to a person when he tries to alter or even compensate for history or how history absorbs rituals into itself and nullifies their effects, and these processes seem naturally and easily enriched by images suggestive of rituals. Bleak as the work may be, the meaning provided by the plot is not imposed on time; rather, the plot is an understandable, recognizable process which, difficult as it may be to accept, is suggestive of those temporal powers by which individual life is overpowered. This image of temporal power is enlarged and not diminished by whatever could be said of Miss Lonelyhearts's innocence, ignorance, emotional confusion, and pride.

The first of the two stories in J. D. Salinger's *Franny and Zooey* is a helpful but not necessary prelude to the second. It renders the occasion of Franny's emotional collapse with which the story Zooey primarily deals. The occasion is a conflict between the delicate and quite spiritual Franny Glass and her fairly worldly young man, Lane. Their football weekend ends by Franny leaving Lane and, apparently, returning home. Lane put Franny off by reducing human actions and relationships to material and social success, to sexual gratification, or to psychological categories. Franny tends to relate human actions and relationships to spiritual disciplines.

Buddy Glass's introduction to Zooey presents the larger Glass setting, particularly the attempt of Buddy and Seymour Glass to teach the younger Zooey and Franny a Zen-like quest for no-knowledge prior to the children's public educational experience. This instruction created in the younger children a kind of orientation which estranged them from their peers and continues to cause them problems, if in no other way than that they are bothered by the fact that it has left them feeling, in some indefinable way, superior to other people. They feel guilty about this feeling, but at the same time they continually find themselves having to judge the attitudes and behavior of other people as unacceptable to them.

The problem of the first part, then, is that both of these young people, and particularly Franny, are distressed by their inability to negotiate a fruitful relationship between themselves and their worlds. A less explicit but important aspect of this problem is that they find themselves, at their age, in their parents' home. That this is a source of their uneasiness, too, is humorously suggested by Zooey's remonstrations toward his mother's invasion of his privacy in the bathroom, by Franny's refusal of her mother's attentions, particularly the chicken soup she has been trying to force on Franny, and by their attitude toward their father. A minor support of this uneasy relation between the action and its setting is that while all of this is going on, the apartment is being worked on by redecorators. The plot is complicated, in other words, by the fact that the children's relation to their origins is largely responsible for the problems they are having, yet their origins are the only place to which they can return in order to be freed from those problems.

The struggles of the second part arise from the confessions the siblings make to one another, their self-accusations, and, particularly, the quite telling criticisms of her attitudes which Franny receives from Zooey. Although they are alike in their common uneasiness about being so different and alienated from other people, about feeling superior to them, they do not rest in the realization of this common dilemma and in mutual pity for one another. Rather, Zooey undercuts Franny's spiritual practices and supplies some ground for an alternative by bringing in to support both of them some of the affirmative wisdom of their older brothers; this he does by reading Buddy's letter, by references to the brothers during the long conversation, and by impersonating Buddy on the phone when Zooey calls Franny from their brothers' bedroom.

Before making the call, Zooey also reads quotations the boys had put on the wall, and he reads parts of Seymour's diary. It is not so much that this reorientation to their older brothers gives specific answers to the problems Franny and Zooey are having in their relationships with other people as that this reassociation seems to have a quickening effect. This allows Zooey to pursue his conversation with Franny and allows her to cope with the criticisms he levels. Most importantly, it provides the basis for their renewed sense of self-worth, purpose, and unity during the phone conversation. The specific occasion for this change in attitude is their mutual recall of Seymour's injunction to shine their shoes for the Fat Lady. The wisdom imbedded in that directive seems directly to apply to the siblings' problems. It involves the discipline of extending one's capacity for acceptance by making the least attractive component of one's world the figure of highest religious authority. Zooey calls the Fat Lady Christ himself, and it is for joy that Franny can hardly hold on to the phone. After listening to the "om" of the dial tone, she replaces the receiver, clears the smoking things away, and, smiling, falls asleep.

The plot of this story renders a process of return to origins with the accompanying experience of renewal. It need hardly be said that the plot is complicated and enriched by religious matters, since the heady spiritual references and acts seem to compel the implied author to compensate for them by detailing the physical movement of the characters, particularly their hand movements, as well as the particulars of the apartment's furnishings and the contents of the—by now famous—closets and pockets.

The spiritual discussions which give meaning to the plot have to do primarily with avoiding spiritual pride. Franny is vulnerable to it because she sentimentalizes religion, failing to realize that Jesus, by loving people rather than animals, did the more difficult thing. Both of these young people must ease the sense of strain which has developed from their awareness of their more refined spiritual and aesthetic sensitivities, the strain of distance consequently felt between themselves and their worlds. This they overcome, but not finally through their brothers' teachings; they overcome it by the process of returning to those origins which had made them different. The risk involved is that this return will make them even more dependent than they already are on those origins, will, also, make them feel even more separate from their worlds, and will allow them to respond to one another in their mutual distress with sentimental pity. What happens instead is that the process of return puts them in contact with a firm base of genuine charity and wisdom, connected with their mother, brothers, and one another. From this new sense of attachment they can extend charity and understanding not only towards people from whom they can receive the satisfaction of recognition and acclaim, but towards the Fat Lady as well.

III

These three fictions, dominated by plots and complicated and enriched by religious imagery and ideas, involve the reader primarily in processes, processes which are not limited in their significance to the specific characters who undergo them. Rather, the plots are intended as imitations or reflections of processes which are possible forms of human time.

This is not a way of saying that the three plots mean the same thing. The first, the plot of *The Spire,* is a rather humanistic, Greek kind of plot,[23] although surely not of a kind that limits it to a specific time or culture. Rather, the character's primary problem, although he had others as well, is that he must act in

23. See Preston T. Roberts, Jr., "A Christian Theory of Dramatic Tragedy," in *The New Orpheus: Essays Toward a Christian Poetic,* ed. Nathan A. Scott (New York: Sheed and Ward, 1964), pp. 255–285, and "Bringing Pathos Into Focus," *Motive* (December, 1953): 7–11, 15. I am also indebted to Mr. Roberts for remarks he made concerning *Miss Lonelyhearts* and *Franny and Zooey* while I was a student in his classes at the University of Chicago.

at least partial ignorance, and the act he feels necessary to complete brings him beyond the boundaries of other human acts, of precedent. For this he suffers. The plot reveals how our acts involve us in events which are beyond our control, and it reveals the consequences of moving from rituals to history. The second, the plot of *Miss Lonelyhearts,* is more skeptical, less humanistic, and the process involves the victimization, perhaps sacrificial in character, of a person whose specific solutions are not only inadequate, but also even disconnected from the problems they are intended to address; it reveals a contrary relation between ritual and history. And in *Zooey* the plot suggests a process which results not in the extension of human possibilities nor in their intimidation, but in the introduction of something new, or renewed, through the charity of support and forgiveness. It reveals the move from history to ritual, the primacy of ritual to history, and the relation of the two to one another.

If Northrop Frye's typology were used, *Miss Lonelyhearts* would be seen as ironic or winter literature, *Zooey* as comic or an example of a plot of spring, and *The Spire* as formed by a tragic or autumn plot. However it is put, the processes expressed by or reflected in these plots are well known, inherently coherent, and variably meaningful kinds of temporal forms. Plots, when they are dominant, tend to be mimetic of these recurring temporal processes in which individuals and groups are involved and by which, willy-nilly, they are carried along.

The plots of fiction, therefore, stand to our ordinary time as, referring back to our opening discussion of Eliade's view of time and myth, the time of myth and ritual stands to history. And the third answer which this chapter is suggesting to the question, Why do narratives have real or potential religious meaning?, is that they do because yet another element of narrative naturally takes to itself associations of a religiously suggestive kind, and the kinds of religious associations plot takes to itself are derived from ritual and the rehearsal of great events in religious life, what Eliade calls repetition.

When Scholes and Kellogg deal with plot, they speak of "plotting" instead, making plot, thereby, a consequence of conscious, authorial intention, a temporal span *given* coherence by an individual's conscious act.[24] But the unique meaning of which plot is capable lies in its suggestion that at least kinds or dimensions of temporal experience can root characters in processes which are not wholly invented and imposed, processes which are in themselves coherent, meaningful, and lifelike.

The difference between "plotting" and plot is nicely suggested by John Barth in *The Sot-Weed Factor*. Toward the end of that book the reader is told:

> . . . we all invent our pasts, more or less, as we go along, at the dictates of Whim and Interest; the happenings of former time are a clay in the present moment that will-we, nill-we, the lot of us must sculpt.[25]

But, as is typical in Barth's work, that opinion of our relation to time is undercut by the story. In the story, the plot is not a result of "plotting" or "sculpting" as much as it is reflective of an actual process. Ebenezer Cooke, living at the end of the seventeenth century, is changed, carried along by forces around him, because, as Barth fully realizes, at that particular moment the times changed, changed in ways that, like it or not, continue largely to determine our lives. The movement of time from before to after Descartes, from a Europe oriented toward classical and Christian traditions to barbaric America, from poetry as related to experience and truth to poetry relegated to a separate sphere—these changes are what carry Ebenezer along on his own move from innocence to experience. The seventeenth century, as George Poulet reminds us, was a time when "the feeling of spontaneous intercommunication in all individual activity with the cosmic *becoming* . . . also disappeared."[26] Consequently, the relation of human consciousness to time was altered:

24. Robert Scholes and Robert Kellogg, *The Nature of Narrative* (New York: Oxford University Press, 1966), p. 218. John Vernon's *The Garden and the Map: Schizophrenia in Twentieth Century Literature and Culture* (Urbana: University of Illinois Press, 1973), a book to which I referred in the preceding chapter, has an interesting discussion of plot in chapter 2. Vernon comments that plot also means a small area of property, and it is his thesis that the realistic novel renders life as charted by an abstract spatial plan and not as life is experienced, namely, temporally.

25. John Barth, *The Sot-Weed Factor* (Garden City: Doubleday and Co., 1960), p. 793.

26. George Poulet, *Studies in Human Time*, trans. Elliott Coleman (Baltimore: Johns Hopkins Press, 1956), p. 13. Cf. also, pp. 13–18.

Separated from the duration of things, and even from that of the modes of its existence, the human consciousness finds itself reduced to existence without duration. It is always of the present moment.[27]

The experience of time became, and continues now to be, a "sense of the discontinuity of duration."[28]

It is this experience of time which Frank Kermode confirms in his study of fictional plots. For him, our being in time is a matter of discontinuous duration, and experience is a matter of "merely sequential" time, unordered, incoherent, and meaningless. In contrast to the experience of time stand plots, consciously constructed fabrications in which time is rendered as ordered concords which never should be taken as imitative of time and our experience of it. Plot for Kermode, as well as for Scholes and Kellogg, is, as I said earlier, dissolved into tone.

We have before us, it appears to me, a fairly major matter for narrative as well as religious theory. Is it indeed the case, for example, that neither fictional plots nor religious rituals have any kind of relation to natural processes of creativity, dissolution, or restoration? I rest the case on the three fictions discussed before. Others that could be cited are the works of people like Thomas Mann, Hermann Hesse, D. H. Lawrence, Ernest Hemingway, and William Faulkner. The status of plot in their work is at least to some degree derived from plot's relation to natural, common human experiences with and in time. Plot does not necessarily give to fiction a temporality which is antithetical to our own experiences of time.

Even if we were able convincingly to establish that plots reflect temporal processes in which we are all involved or which we all experience, a second, major matter would still need to be addressed, namely, the relation of these recurring natural, psychic, or social processes to linear time, a time defined by new, nonrecoverable, and nonrepeatable occurrences.

This problem has its counterpart in religious discussions. Biblical religions and the history of Judaism and Christianity have had within them tensions between cyclical and linear time. On the one hand are the yearly celebrations, the church year in

27. Ibid., p. 13.
28. Ibid., p. 16.

Christian worship, for example. The Jewish Passover or the Christian Eucharist are repeated acts in which the time of their origination is opened to access by participants; Jewish celebrants really come out of Egypt and Christians really stand in the presence of Jesus. But equally if not more important is history, charged, according to Israel and the Christian church, with the divine power to bring it to a meaningful goal. It is this linear side, the religious understanding of history, that Poulet, Kermode, et al. are pointing to as problematic. This loss is particularly felt by Jewish thinkers for whom the holocaust marks a dead end to attempts to see history as the unfolding of divine intention. If anything is left to the enterprise of viewing time as religiously meaningful, it is to be found, as with Rabbi Rubenstein, in ritual or cyclical time.[29]

Literary theorists and theologians, then, are faced with a similar problem. First, each must explore the meaning of temporality within the forms of their respective domains, the time of plots and the time of rituals, to determine whether and how that time is related to recurring natural, psychic, or social processes. But then they have another and more difficult problem in common, namely, to discern the relation between the time of ritual or the time of plot, as the case may be, and linear time, what Kermode calls "sequential time" and Eliade the "terror of history."

Some theologians and theorists of religion are trying to come to terms with this latter problem, and they are trying to handle it by avoiding limiting religiously meaningful time to religious rituals and by avoiding isolating religiously meaningful time to discrete moments and events.[30] John Dunne, for example, has explored the possibility of seeing linear time as religiously meaningful by inverting the certainties as they are given us, for example, in Kermode. Dunne contends that the time which is most obvious to us, of which we are most conscious, is cyclical time, time related to bodily and psychological processes. Even passage

29. See Richard L. Rubenstein, *After Auschwitz: Radical Theology and Contemporary Judaism* (Indianapolis: Bobbs-Merrill Co., 1966) and idem, "Judaism and the Death of God," *Playboy* (July, 1967): 74.

30. These attempts are post-Bultmannian and post-Niebuhrian in their attempts to move beyond the event orientation of both of these theologians. See, e.g., Rudolf Bultmann, *Jesus Christ and Mythology* (New York: Charles Scribner's Sons, 1958), esp. chapter 2, and H. Richard Niebuhr, *The Meaning of Revelation* (New York: Macmillan Co., 1962).

through stages of life and into advanced years is available to consciousness as a natural, recurring process. What is not so obvious and what is highly meaningful for a person is what is linear, and he proposes that linear time and its meaning are related to cyclical time and its meaning as overtone is related to tone. Rather than being less meaningful and personal as with Kermode, linear time for Dunne is potentially more meaningful, and it is linear time which gives rise to our individuality, our unique version of the human story. Plots, rituals, and processes give the tones to life stories; linear, individual time gives the overtones. Although Dunne's theory has a tendency to slide the emphasis of narrative time toward tone, in the sense I am using that term in this study, it at least has the advantage of inverting Kermode's categories and suggesting a set of new possibilities.[31]

Another post-Bultmannian theorist is Herbert Richardson. After remarking that we tend to employ the image of the story when we reflect on our lives, Richardson claims that we are not fully in control as to what kind of story we make our lives out to be. We are determined by three plots or myths which shape our life stories: separation and return, conflict and vindication, and internal actualization.[32] By relating the first of these to infancy, the second to adolescence, and the third to maturity, Richardson mars his study by a rhetorical strategy that allows him implicitly to undercut the validity of two of these stories. Despite this fault, the presentation interestingly suggests why and how it is true that we are guided as we think of the temporal dimension of our lives; human time is determined by plots which are not forced on time but are to be perceived as constitutive of our awareness of time.

Sam Keen puts the matter more personally when he suggests that it is the presence of promises and commitment that gives the temporal process in which we find ourselves, meaning and power —promises which come first of all to us and then from us. A

31. John S. Dunne, *Time and Myth* (Garden City: Doubleday and Co., 1973), esp. pp. 21–23.
32. Herbert W. Richardson, "Three Myths of Transcendence," in *Transcendence*, ed. Herbert Richardson and Donald Cutler (Boston: Beacon Press, 1969), pp. 98–113. The last of these plots is very similar to that kind of process which Jerry Bryant detects in his study of American literature and which he advocates. See Jerry H. Bryant, *The Open Decision: The Contemporary American Novel and Its Intellectual Background* (New York: Free Press, 1970).

person's time can be seen as meaningful when viewed as constituted, at least in part, of acts which are intended toward him by
people who have made promises or are in other ways committed
to him. He says, "Each of us is redeemed from shallow and hostile life by the sacrificial love and civility which we have gratuitously received."[33] Although it is impossible to explain why people extend themselves in this way toward others, the result is
that a temporal structure arises which has its source and meaning outside of our control and expectation. People make promises and commitments, and our time is made thereby meaningful
and coherent. When a person, from youth up, is the recipient of
promises and commitments, he is enabled to act in the same way
toward others; "I seek to manifest that same faithfulness toward
others which was gratuitously shown to me," he says.[34] In the
story of promises and commitments made and met, lies a person's story, the story of how we are made human.

Finally, attention should be called to Stephen Crites's attempt
to establish the narrative quality of experience as not projected
onto human life, but inherent in it. His basic point is that consciousness is created by story, and not story by consciousness.
For example, the stories that are told in traditional societies are
only approximations of the real story, for the real story is not so
much in consciousness as it is "in the arms and legs and bellies
of the celebrants."[35] When consciousness is "wrenched out of
story," it either is victimized by uninterpreted particulars and
events or elevates itself above them; in either case a consciousness that is cut off from story is diseased, "seized by desiccated
abstractions and scatological immediacies."[36]

These are a few theologians or theorists of religion who are
trying to deal with the meaningfulness of linear time without
going back to earlier formulations of providence and without
limiting themselves to a meaningful relation to particular moments and events. For all of them in differing ways, the relation
of cyclical to linear time, of ritual, process, or plot to sequence
is a matter of interdependence. Overtones for Dunne, our own

33. Sam Keen, *To A Dancing God* (New York: Harper & Row, 1970).
34. Ibid., p. 102.
35. Stephen Crites, "The Narrative Quality of Experience," *Journal of
the American Academy of Religion* (September, 1971): 295.
36. Ibid., p. 310.

story for Richardson, human promises for Keen, and consciousness for Crites are tied to or arise from something more common, basic, and repeated—the processes we share and which are released in their own power and meaning in rituals and plots.

4

Tone and Belief

I

In recent years tone, the final narrative element, has been asked to carry greater weight and has received more critical attention than any of the other elements. Tone is taken now by many to be always the dominant narrative element; whether as "world view" or "vision" or "sense of life," or even recently, again, "intention,"[1] the image of subjectivity, the image in the work of the author or of the creative act, is taken as the central matter. The first thing that must be said, then, is that tone need not be the most important element in a particular narrative, that fictions can be powerful and meaningful in ways other than through the work's created subjective presence.

A second problem in theory concerning tone is that tone often is only partially viewed. For example, tone is studied only under point of view, as though, so to speak, the physical attitude of the writer or narrator in relation to his material is always of dominant importance.[2] Or the emotional attitude of the writer is isolated, his techniques for providing "the emotional shades that color the sense of his words."[3] Or the matter is handled under

1. See Irving Howe, *A World More Attractive: A View of Modern Literature and Politics* (New York: Horizon Press, 1963); Nathan A. Scott, Jr., *Modern Literature and the Religious Frontier* (New York: Harper and Brothers, 1958); Arthur Mizener, *The Sense of Life in the Modern Novel* (Boston: Houghton Mifflin Co., 1964); and E. D. Hirsch, *Validity in Interpretation* (New Haven: Yale University Press, 1967).

2. See Percy Lubbock, *The Craft of Fiction* (New York: Viking Press, 1960 [originally published in 1921]).

3. Robert Scholes, *The Elements of Fiction* (New York: Oxford University Press, 1968), p. 29.

the rubric of fictional rhetoric.[4] Or tone is treated as style. This last option is particularly problematic, for, in addition to treating tone incompletely, the discussion of style is confused by uncertainty as to what the word means, even though it seems an attractive object for study because it can be handled with an almost scientific objectivity. The meaning of the word shifts, however. Often it means word choice,[5] which can be studied with the aid of computers; but the term can also refer to the highly elusive quality of the work's language. Style can, as it is by Roland Barthes and Leslie Fiedler,[6] be used as a term to indicate what is individuating about a literary work in the sense of the writer's peculiar set of limitations, gifts, and interests, while for others the term suggests precisely what in a work is most consciously created, most clearly the product of authorial effort.

A third problem connected with tone arises from the fact that a few very influential artists and theorists like Henry James, James Joyce, and T. S. Eliot tried to diminish the element of tone, to equate the creative act and the merit of a particular work with its lack of subjective presence. The impersonal theory of literature sees the illusion of reality threatened by hints of authorial presence. Norman Friedman, for example, treats the history of narrative into the twentieth century as an evolution toward the perfection of the form, and what he means by its perfection is the attainment in narrative of its only kind of truth, namely, "story-illusion."[7] Such veneration of author *absconditus* brings its inevitable counterpart into being, the insistence that the principal aesthetic matter in a work is the personal relation between the author and the reader.[8] To repeat and to take a

4. See Wayne C. Booth, *The Rhetoric of Fiction* (Chicago: University of Chicago Press, 1961).

5. As with David Lodge, *Language and Fiction: Essays in Criticism and Verbal Analysis of the English Novel* (New York: Columbia University Press, 1966).

6. Roland Barthes, *Writing Degree Zero*, trans. Annette Lavers and Colin Smith with a preface by Susan Sontag (New York: Hill and Wang, 1967), p. 13 and Leslie Fiedler, *No! In Thunder* (London, Eyre and Spottiswoode, 1963).

7. Norman Friedman, "Point of View in Fiction: The Development of a Critical Concept," in *The Theory of the Novel*, ed. Philip Stevick (New York: Free Press, 1967), pp. 108–138.

8. Walter J. Ong, *The Barbarian Within and Other Fugitive Essays and Studies* (New York: Macmillan Co., 1962).

position in relation to all of this: Tone has three aspects, which I shall discuss later; tone is always present in a narrative; and tone need not be the dominant element of a particular fiction.

Finally, Scholes and Kellogg introduce a major matter when they suggest that for philosophical reasons tone tends to be a less important element than it may once have been. This is due to the fact, they argue, that in a relativistic age like our own an author cannot create an image of himself that readers will readily accept as an authority. The status of tone is deeply undermined by the fact that "all our nonliterary sources of knowledge and understanding, which is to say the natural and social sciences with philosophy and theology trailing along behind, led us to see truth, beauty, and goodness as relative rather than absolute matters."[9] Scholes and Kellogg appear to chide Wayne Booth for his uneasiness with unreliable narrators, seeing his impatience as a nostalgia for a time when someone else's opinions or beliefs about material would make more of a difference to the reader. In addition, it should be seen that Scholes and Kellogg tend to shift the authority to objective fact, since they treat point of view primarily as a way of opening and closing information sources; subjective opinion and belief are reduced for them in the presence of the authority of objective fact.

The literary empiricism of Scholes and Kellogg finds a heavy counterpart in the rise of the "criticism of consciousness." Under its influence a primacy is granted the creative consciousness, and a fictional work becomes thought of as a mental universe dominated by "each writer's special 'tone.' "[10] It is the personal quality of literature, the subjective ordering of experience, that constitutes the literary act and the principal matter for critical attention. Whether taking a structuralist form by relating this ordering of experience to mental patterns[11] or an existentialist form by seeing consciousness not as diminishing itself in the face of relativity, but exercising its autonomy in that

9. Robert Scholes and Robert Kellogg, *The Nature of Narrative* (New York: Oxford University Press, 1966), p. 276.
10. Sarah N. Lawall, *Critics of Consciousness: The Existential Structure of Literature* (Cambridge: Harvard University Press, 1968), p. 10.
11. See Jacques Ehrmann, ed., *Structuralism* (Garden City: Doubleday and Co., 1966), pp. 137–239 and Vernon W. Gras, ed., *European Literary Theory and Practice: From Existential Phenomenology to Structuralism* (New York: Dell Publishing Co., 1973).

situation, this emphasis places more burden on tone than Scholes and Kellogg take away.

Furthermore, critics of contemporary fiction such as Richard Poirier and Tony Tanner add to this discussion their own kind of accent on tone. For Poirier, the characteristic of recent literature most worthy of note is the image of personal energy, the performing self in the act of fighting through "the glitter and rubbish" of contemporary experience in order to express something worthwhile.[12] And Tony Tanner is talking about tone when he takes as a presiding effect of recent American fiction the "reflection or projection of the author's sense of his own situation among words."[13]

Rather than see the possibilities of narrative determined by philosophical and psychological interests and theories, I would urge that tone is no more affected by modern shifts of orientation and formulations than are the other elements, and I think I have indicated what is happening to them during this period as well. Also, although a philosophical or sociological theory, or any other kind of theory for that matter, may give a critic particular insights into narrative theory that he would not otherwise have, I think it is important for him to resist any conclusion or any limitation of his work to a theory which would force him to discount narrative possibilities from the start.

A balance between tone and the other elements, however, may not be so easy to maintain. Is it not true, for example, that tone drags everything into itself, since a fictional world is a highly personal, and consequently idiosyncratic, world? Although the other elements seem to stand on their own two feet, so to speak, are they not still the author's atmosphere, characters, and plot? We have Camus' Oran, Greene's Querry, and Golding's tragic plot, do we not? Although in one sense this is so, in another important way it is not. Although a fictional world is an author's invention and is consequently tied to the subjective presence in the work, a fictional world is also more than one person's world. In a fiction, particularly when tone is not domi-

12. Richard Poirier, *The Performing Self: Compositions and Decompositions in the Language of Contemporary Life* (New York: Oxford University Press, 1971), p. 11.

13. Tony Tanner, *City of Words: American Fiction, 1950–1970* (New York: Harper & Row, 1971), p. 18.

nant, a claim can be made on us to engage in a hermeneutical act which will allow the special authority and autonomy of one or more of the other elements to exert its sway. To enter a fictional world unprepared to believe that such and such is so, and so not simply because the implied author thinks it is, is to be unprepared for entering a fictional world. To insist that all assumptions, assertions, and values are subjective projections—to insist, that is, on taking that view into the reading—is to undercut the power of the other elements and their potential meaning. To imagine oneself into a fictional world is to be prepared, if only for a few hours, to accept, if asked to, someone's fictional world as a state of affairs.

Of course, we can and often do find ourselves in fictions dominated by tone; they tend to be what Northrop Frye calls confessional fictions. Perhaps, in fact, it could be argued that what Frye means by the forms of fiction are actually kinds of fictions in which one rather than some other of the elements of narrative holds a dominant position. In any event, it must also be said that Frye unnecessarily limits the possibilities of the confessional form when he thinks of it as arising primarily from the image of a subjective presence which discloses itself because of its struggle with some significant problem in "religion, politics, or art,"[14] a struggle which allows the narrator to think of his life as worth writing about. This possibility indeed is often active in fiction, and I attempted at one point to reveal how in the works of five recent American writers the problem of marginality, of being on the margins of two worlds but belonging wholly to neither one, was addressed by them and how the specific forms of this struggle gave the narrators of these fictions a sense of the urgency about their lives.[15] But there is another kind of confessional fiction, namely, a fiction arising from the narrator's or implied author's desire to bear witness to some significant place, event,

14. Northrop Frye, *Anatomy of Criticism* (New York: Atheneum, 1966), p. 308.
15. See Wesley A. Kort, *Shriven Selves: Religious Problems in Recent American Fiction* (Philadelphia: Fortress Press, 1972). By "marginal," here, I do not mean what is usually indicated in literary criticism by that term, namely, life outside of or prior to society—Frederick J. Hoffman, *Marginal Manners: The Variants of Bohemia* (Evanston and New York: Row, Peterson and Co., 1962). I mean by "marginal" what Everett Stonequist makes of the term in his book, *The Marginal Man* (New York: Charles Scribner's Sons, 1937).

or, most often, person—something, in short, by which the narrator has been deeply affected or even changed. This is the case in such recent American fictions as John Knowles's *A Separate Peace,* William Styron's *Set This House on Fire,* Peter De Vries's *The Blood of the Lamb,* and Jack Kerouac's *Visions of Gerard.* Of course, it must also be said that to the degree that tone forces attention on some place, person, or events that are important to the narrator, to that degree the emphasis begins to pass over to one or more of the other elements.

Before turning to examples of tone-dominated fictions, one more thing should be said about tone, namely, that it has three aspects: selection of material, language choice, and attitude—attitude in both a physical and emotional-intellectual sense. The writer chooses to tell us about something, he uses a kind of language or uses language in a certain way, and he has or assumes a certain attitude or set of attitudes toward what he is telling the reader. Now, of course, these three aspects of tone are not sepparate things; they are together in one act, and we should be sufficiently aware of the kind of theoretical direction that Roland Barthes or Maurice Merleau-Ponty provide to avoid separating subject matter, language, and personal investment from one another.[16] Tone cannot be taken as the way in which material has been dressed up (or dressed down!) in language. It is the need to speak which leads to what can and must be said, and it is something to be named or some attitude to be expressed that leads to speaking. Material and attitude toward it are not related to one another as handle is related to gripping; the material forms the attitude, and the attitude affects the material. Tone, then, is an image of the creative act, and the creative act is the moment in which material, language, and attitude arise as one thing.

The three examples of tone-dominated fiction may be viewed in such a way as to suggest that in each of them one rather than the other two aspects of tone seems most important. In *Cat and Mouse* the emphasis seems to fall on that aspect of tone I called the selection of material; *Too Late The Phalarope* places a bit more emphasis on finding adequate and appropriate language;

16. Barthes, *Writing Degree Zero,* particularly pp. 13–20 and Maurice Merleau-Ponty, *Signs,* trans. Richard C. McCleary (Evanston, Ill.: Northwestern University Press, 1964), particularly pp. 53–71.

and *A Death in the Family* attracts attention to the attitude of the narrator toward his material. To repeat, these emphases do not exclude the other aspects of tone, and I call attention to them only by way of illustrating how tone has these various aspects or sides.

II

The narrator of Günter Grass's *Cat and Mouse* is as much selected by his material as he is the selector of it. The material, a period during the narrator's boyhood and, particularly, his friendship with young Joachim Mahlke, has had a hold on the narrator throughout his life, and writing about it is a way of coming to terms with it. The hold results from the mysteriousness of this boyhood friend, and the ambivalence of Pilenz toward him results in spiritual quandaries. Still, despite these ambiguities, the tone is one of celebration, an expression of indebtedness, and the novel is an example of a confessional fiction which arises not so much from the results of working through a problem, although some of that is present also, as from the desire to bear witness to the weight and mystery of the "separate peace" over which Joachim Mahlke presided.

Pilenz as a youth stood in amazement of Joachim. In fact, Pilenz has never fully recovered from Mahlke's departure. This estimation of Mahlke's value, however, produces a corresponding guilt in Pilenz because at the time the narrator had been unable to show Mahlke just how important he considered Mahlke to be to him. In fact, it appears that Pilenz has been working as secretary in a settlement house primarily to assuage his guilt. The narration is a literary pilgrimage back to that former time and commanding person, and the selection of material is both for the purpose of overcoming the guilt and expressing the admiration and indebtedness which Pilenz failed adequately to express to Mahlke in person.

The four parts present stages in Mahlke's development. From an awkward weakling he advances to a position of leadership among his peers, to a trickster figure and hero, and he finally becomes an antagonist to social and cosmic forces. Throughout his career, however, Mahlke himself, Pilenz seems now to recognize, was a lonely young man.

Pilenz, while fascinated by Mahlke, resents him, too, primarily because Mahlke reminds him of his own inadequacies. Pilenz has several problems: his prostitute mother, his inability to believe or to worship, his incapacity to respond emotionally to his brother's death, and his severe lack of confidence in his own masculinity. In contrast stand Mahlke's bravery, physical strength, and skills; Pilenz resents as much as he admires Mahlke, and the cat is an image of Pilenz's complicity in the vengeance on his friend for reminding Pilenz of his own inadequacies.

Mahlke develops his skills and strengths with an awareness of the evils around him. He knows what exclusion is, since his earlier weaknesses and his grotesque Adam's apple guaranteed him no social position, and he works his way to becoming high priest of the boys' summer exploits in order to overcome exclusion. He seems to be more aware than his friends are of evils around their circle of freedom. Finally, we learn that Mahlke is religiously insecure because of his father's death without benefit of the sacrament, and Mahlke's life and spiritual devotion may be seen as compensations for his father's death.

From the beginning the boys identify war and sports with each other. This identification is reinforced by the visit to the school of a military pilot who speaks of fighting as though it were a game. Mahlke decides to extend his activity, then, from the sunken barge to the larger military world. A second visitor to the school, a U-boat captain, supports this link between war and sports; Mahlke decides to become a military hero.

As he extends his activities, Mahlke deepens his private, religious life. He prepares in the radio shack of the submerged ship a chapel-hideaway for himself and the Virgin, an act which Pilenz, the only other Catholic in the group, understands. Mahlke becomes more daring in his exploits, particularly stealing the captain's Knight's Cross and dancing naked with it on the barge. In the military his exploits become a legend: his liturgical graffiti on the bathroom walls, his sexual services to the commander's wife, and his scores on Russian tanks. Mahlke climaxes this stage of his development by returning to his school with a Knight's Cross of his own, a return significant to him because he plans to use the occasion to tell the boys that his success in the war was due to visits by the Virgin carrying a picture with her of his father. It was at the locomotive which killed his father that he was aiming, not at Russian tanks. But

Mahlke is prevented from making this speech, and when this happens his world falls apart.

Presumably on the Friday before Palm Sunday, the liturgical material of Palm Sunday having been Mahlke's favorite throughout, Pilenz accompanies Mahlke on his last trip to the barge. Pilenz goes along reluctantly and on the way tells Mahlke a lie, namely, that the police had been searching for Mahlke. Despite Pilenz's viciousness, however, Mahlke is happy. He goes under the water, and he does not surface again. The narration ends in silence. Pilenz has been awaiting Mahlke's return; trickster figures should reappear, but there has been nothing to fill the void left by the departure.

Pilenz's youth and his relation to Mahlke are ambiguous because of the inappropriate attitudes the boys had towards war. On the one hand, they tended to mechanize and quantify it, thinking of it in terms not of people, but of equipment; on the other hand, they tended to personalize it, domesticating it in metaphors taken from sports. The atmosphere in which these boys live, rife with indications of war and structured by athletic achievements, makes human relationships of a creative and supportive nature very difficult. The boys tend to be competitive with each other, to underestimate evil around them, and to mistake the level at which their own acts of thoughtlessness or aggression can strike home.

Complicating the matter still further is Mahlke's relation to the Virgin. Of special importance is the Black Madonna of Czestochowa, whose image Mahlke wears and to whom he turns at the end. Believed to have been painted by St. Luke, associated with healing, and credited with protection of the Polish people in war, the Black Madonna is an important object of pilgrimage. But the healing and protection in war which she finally affords Mahlke is to be found in his own watery death.

The object of Pilenz's pilgrimage—Mahlke—is, consequently, a mysterious figure, and the attitude of the narrator toward him is quite complex. Pilenz makes a literary testimony to Mahlke which combines his own estimation of what was wrongheaded and pathetic in that situation with what was joyful and free, what was spiritually renewing and promising with what was regressive, what deserved support and celebration with what deserved rebuke. Even more, Mahlke's disappearance has not been compensated for by any new appearance of an enlivening, defiant, and community-creating trickster, and the narrative is colored by the poignance of realizing that we often recognize the value of people only after our relation with them has been terminated. But Mahlke's absence has allowed Pilenz to embark on his own reappropriation of the complex materials of his history. Mahlke is never so well known, understood, and appreciated as he is in his absence. The material with which the narrator primarily deals, then, is the material of absence, of silence, and it is this which makes the selection of Mahlke as the principal object of his narration so ambiguous an act.

Although the narrator of Alan Paton's *Too Late the Phalarope* is also engaged by an effort to testify to the importance of a particular figure and set of events, the particularly noticeable aspect of the tone in this work is not quite so much the selection of material as it is the effort to use language. Tante Sophie has difficulty with language because of physical, cultural, and personal handicaps, and her limitations suggest a more general failure to account fully for such events, a failure that cannot wholly be attributed to her awkwardness. The material with which she is dealing not only has sides hidden from public view, but it also has sides that seem inherently inexplicable. In addition, Tante Sophie, despite her limitations, tells this story by way of asserting that she herself was to a degree responsible for what happened to Pieter and his family.

That Tante Sophie's attempt to deal with the hidden complexities of the events falls short of doing justice to what is involved can be seen in at least two ways. First, she is not as attentive as the implied author apparently intends the reader to be to the ambiguities of the social situation, particularly the forced separation of people from one another according to race and the clear elevation of the whites above the blacks. This situation begs for redress, if only that the claims of the excluded and forbidden majority make themselves felt in subtle if not overt ways. Second, Tante Sophie has too high an opinion of her own real or potential importance to Pieter. No one in her story takes her as seriously as she would have to be taken if her word to Pieter or other kind of help were to have had the effect she imagines in averting the catastrophe. Furthermore, Sophie seems to think of herself as potentially a better mother or better wife to Pieter than those he has, and, if she thinks this, it is because, unmarried and disfigured, she desires those positions so deeply and discounts the ambiguities inherent in them. Sophie is, then, a narrator who complicates the events with insights and feelings not otherwise open to public view, and, because of limitations both in language and personal experience, falls short of dealing adequately with her material.

Pieter's behavior is not, of course, wholly explicable. He has both virile and delicate sides, and he is a gifted person, although he seems to unduly limit his horizons to a fairly low-level police job, popular classical music, philately, and rugby. He enjoys the recognition that some of his success grants him, although he seems bent on punishing himself for that elevation. And he harbours resentment toward his wife for the uneasiness with sex that her culture has taught her, a resentment that allows him to enter the forbidden affair with Stephanie. The forbidden act results in as much pain as satisfaction for him, and it puts him into a position of allowing her to pull down his entire world and that of those immediately around him. What is most deeply enigmatic, however, is what Sophie refers to as his *swaartgalligheid,* his retreat into self-pity and resentment, a retreat which he seems to enjoy and in which, perhaps too, he seems most like himself. His relation with others and his social successes are, in contrast, quite insecure excursions and tentative connections compared to the dark, emotional corner into which he retreats and from which his destructive acts arise.

The insecure and tentative nature of his personal relations is suggested by the way the story is told and by Pieter's actual contacts. We know from the outset that catastrophe will come, and all of his moves away from that event lack the force and inevitability of every move toward it. In addition, of course, his contacts with people are awry. First, he has antagonized Steyn. Although the captain seems capable of a closer relation to Pieter, his commendation comes late in the process toward the inevitable destruction. Vos, the pastor, is in no condition to relate supportively to Pieter because of his own need to have Pieter be a certain kind of man. Perhaps he could have confided more in his cousin Anna, but he allows himself primarily only to be titillated by her. And Kappie, who seems capable of more, is not granted access to Pieter's inner life. Most of all, of course, Pieter has had no real relation to his father. The unfortunate separation in the family of the uncritical love of the mother from the demanding will of the dominant father is typical of the larger social setting and largely responsible for Pieter's personal insecurity. But most of all, the relation with Stephanie seems so forceful, unavoidable, and desirable because it speaks of a reality hidden, repressed, and feared by the dominant, white group. To the degree to which his acceptable relations are tentative and fragile, the relation to Stephanie seems firm and commanding.

Because she gives us more that is problematic in her story than her solution of a closer relation to Pieter could begin to solve, Sophie unintentionally undercuts her authority. While the reader can have respect for her sincerity and can appreciate her many valid insights into the situation, the self-created irony in which the narrator is established has an effect which Paton could not have gained had he had as narrator a person who, with theological, sociological, and psychological sophistication, could have gone much further than Sophie in his analysis and interpretation of this family and their misfortunes. Of course, by the text's being underdetermined, the reader is involved in the process of adding his own assessment of Sophie's perspective on the matter; but more importantly, the failure of the speaker to match up to the demands of the occasion creates a sense of the tension between material and language and, even more, between the unrecognized and uncontrolled ground of social and psychological forces which lie beneath what is apparent. What is wrong and out of control is the entire situation, and Tante Sophie's sincere admission of failure is a poignantly, even pathetically inaccurate and superficial assessment of what it would take to avoid the inevitable consequences.

The most noticeable aspect of tone in James Agee's *A Death in the Family* is the narrator's attitude toward what he gives the reader. What he shares primarily is the high value he places on the family, particularly its ability to absorb shock, the kind of shock the narrator perceives as characteristic of human experience. The attitude of the narrator is one of reverence toward the family under stress, but it is a reverence more generally toward human life revealed to be, in its ability to withstand gratuitous affliction, a noble, mysterious, and resilient thing.

The three parts of the narration are as much topically distinguished as chronologically arranged. In the first, innocence and security dominate: the intimacy between Rufus and his father, the early breakfast Mary prepares for Jay, and Rufus's delight with his new hat. Sentimentality is avoided because the narrator suggests some problems of relationship within the family: Jay's mistrust of his brother, Mary's difficulties with Jay's father, the conflicting attitudes of Jay and Mary toward comical and sexual things, and Jay's refusal to participate in Mary's church affiliation.

The second part deals with the catastrophe and the threatening problems it creates. The most obvious problem, of course, is death—one's own death, the death of someone else, and the sorrow caused by the loss of someone loved. However, it is the gratuitous, undeserved quality of death which presents more of a problem. Agee spares little to underscore the fact that of all persons who should live, this needed, loved, and highly regarded man of thirty-six should live. Finally, the gratuitous, violent character of death puts strain on inherited responses to dying. Andrew enters saying, "And you can still believe in that idiotic God of yours?" Not only does this constitute a problem or crisis of belief, but it also becomes a problem by threatening to divide the family into believers and nonbelievers. The responses to the problems which begin to emerge in this part reinforce one another. First, death is seen as forcing attention back on Jay's life: "In his strength." Death, particularly gratuitous death, reveals, by contrast, the force and beauty of life. In addition, the loss of another, grief, is interpreted by Hannah as forming a discipline for Mary's development of psychic strength. Third, the invasion of the family by this hostile power brings them together. Through talk, laughter, and silence they absorb the event.

In the third part these responses to the death are fully actualized. When Father Jackson arrives, Mary has already begun to take a less religious or traditional attitude, and she does not side with him. Although Mary continues to use the word "God" in her reflections on the matter, the word seems more to suggest a new strength and tenderness within herself than a power outside or beyond.

The response of natural strength and grace to the problems of sorrow, suffering, and death takes on an almost religious quality at the end, however—especially in the butterfly scene. Prior to that moment, resilience and human strength possessed the quality of permanence while evil and God's actions were thought of as gratuitous; now evil is constant—Jay lies in darkness—while beauty, the butterfly, and the sun are the surprise. This religious character of natural or human responses to human problems is also suggested by the kind of preparatory work religious ideas play in relation to nonreligious responses. Religion, by appearing as artificial and divisive in this situation of natural cohesion, is set up as objectionable; it takes on itself the anger and frustration of these deeply hurt people. In addition, by taking this on itself, religion allows the ethic of endurance and human solidarity to stand unexamined. Finally, the more human or natural responses fill in gaps created by a no longer used religious language. For example, Andrew senses the peace of the town late at night because the Christmas carol that adumbrates the experience creates the need for some kind of advent. The butterfly is impressive quite explicitly because of Father Jackson, and the sense of Jay's continued presence in the house may easily be attributed to the spiritual expectation of eternal life. Religion enhances the status of nonreligious responses by absorbing the anger aroused by the event, by allowing these nontraditional responses to go unchallenged, and by preparing a place for them in the capacity for spiritual response.

Tone is particularly noticeable in this narrative, then, as an attitude toward the material. This is not to denigrate the importance of the material and the delicate language Agee employs. It is clear, however, that the narrator returns to these people to admire them, particularly to admire them for epitomizing what is a central truth of human life, namely, that it is most to be valued when it is most violated, and it is most violated in the moment of that blow on the head, that affront to life's dignity, death.

III

Tone, the image of the creative act in the fictional world, supplies that world with a necessary element, so that the conditions of life, the range of human possibilities, and time not only can be established and brought into relation to one another, but perceived and affirmed to be a whole. Tone brings into the fictional world the quality of belief. As one literary theorist puts it:

> The artist subjectively senses the peaks and abysses of human experience and finds himself imaginatively playing with the variety of lines that may unite valley with valley or peak with peak or symbolize their alteration and duration. What he arrives at is . . . a world that is not verifiable through any process of scientific method, but is simply a manifestation of belief.[17]

Professor Wright's essay on tone is, among other things, a commentary on Joseph Conrad's statement, "In truth every novelist must begin by creating for himself a world, great or little, in which he can honestly believe."[18]

Tone, the element of narrative which is the image of that creative moment when choice of material, attitude toward it, and the use of language dance as one, implies, first of all, relation. Relation, when reflected upon, can become a religiously suggestive category. One thinks particularly of Martin Buber's immensely influential relational theology formulated upon his famous "I-Thou" dyad. When material and one's attitude toward it are seen as nondetermining yet wholly complementary to one another not only is their own essential relation perceived, but the "Eternal Thou" is also felt to be hovering about them.[19]

Second, tone suggests wholeness, a fictional world of many dimensions perceived or affirmed to be constituted of parts to some degree related to one another. Wholeness suggests both completeness and unity. If an element of narrative has been slighted we can judge the work as not only incomplete, but also as not whole; the elements of narrative need one another. If elements are inappropriately related to one another we can judge the work to be incoherent; the elements of a narrative should be related to one another, should suggest a whole. Wholeness is a

17. Walter F. Wright, "Tone in Fiction," in *The Theory of the Novel: New Essays*, ed. John Halperin (New York: Oxford University Press, 1974), p. 299.
18. Ibid., p. 298.
19. Martin Buber, *I and Thou*, trans. Ronald Gregor Smith (New York: Charles Scribner's Sons, 1958), particularly, pp. 75–120.

universal which, if it has any meaning at all, suggests a kind of experience, a sense of the way things are, namely, that however undemonstrable the contention or hypothesis may be, things of this world are taken to constitute a whole in some way analogous to the "whole" one can call an aesthetic work, complete, unified. To say such a thing of one's world is to make a kind of religious affirmation, a fact to which, among others, Herbert Richardson points when he calls the feeling of wholeness or fittingness the "object" of religious experience.[20] This is the kind of thing to which Clifford Geertz points when he calls a religious attitude toward the world one in which the ethical and the metaphysical are united, one in which what *is,* is as it ought to be.[21] To the degree to which it is the case that relation and wholeness are kinds of experiences which are religiously suggestive or symptomatic of religious life, it would not be surprising that tone would attract to itself associations of a religiously suggestive kind, particularly now of a kind related to the act of affirmation or the experience of belief, and even more particularly, to the sense of relation and wholeness.

Now we are in a position to deal with a point that those familiar with the emphasis on the primacy of language in literature may have for some time been impatient to take up, for it is in language that the peculiar nature of relationship and unity is to be perceived. To put it differently, by returning to the three aspects of tone, it must be said that it is by language that material choice and attitude toward it are related, unified. Language in relation to material choice and attitude is somewhat like the present in relation to the past and the future; it is the principal matter, but it is also the most elusive. As the present keeps get-

20. Herbert W. Richardson, "Three Myths of Transcendence," in *Transcendence,* ed. Herbert Richardson and Donald Cutler (Boston: Beacon Press, 1969). In the same volume, see Robert N. Bellah, "Transcendence in Contemporary Piety." Bellah argues that symbols of transcendence are symbols of the world experienced as a whole, symbols by which the tension of otherness in self, society, and nature is overcome in wholeness.
21. Clifford Geertz, "Ethos, World View, and the Analysis of Sacred Symbols," in his *The Interpretation of Cultures* (New York: Basic Books, 1973). "Sacred symbols thus relate an ontology and a cosmology to an aesthetics and a morality: their peculiar power comes from their presumed ability to identify fact with value at the most fundamental level, to give to what is otherwise merely actual, a comprehensive normative import" (p. 127).

ting talked about in terms of the past and the future, so the language of a narrative, while in a sense the only "reality" of a fiction, is talked about in terms of material choice and attitude. Finally, the language of fiction points to silence, to what in material cannot be expressed in language and to what in attitude cannot wholly be actualized in words.

The language of a narrative, then, has silence on two sides of it—the material and the attitude. These silences give language its legitimacy and its meaning, but they also intimidate it. Anyone may have had the experience of material both legitimizing and intimidating language; we find ourselves occasionally in a situation fraught with meaning, a time in which something very painful or something unusually joyful has happened. It is on such occasions that we most deeply feel that something ought to be said. It is often on just such occasions, however, that we have that sinking feeling of wanting, needing to say something and being at a loss for words—or worse yet, of having said something inadequate or even inappropriate. In addition, and at the same time, we may have a model in our minds of what it would be like to give expression to the perfect attitude at such a time, a model of the totally adequate judge and speaker for the occasion: "If Pat were here, he would say the right thing!" or "Milton! thou shouldst be living at this hour:/England hath need of thee . . . / Thou hadst a voice whose sound was like the sea. . . ." The image of a perfect attitude, of a Daniel to judge, of a Joseph to speak before this Pharoah, intimidates language, but it also inspires it, helps us in forming attitudes and choosing words. Models of wholly adequate words legitimize the act of speaking, suggesting that it may be possible to say the right thing, to find language adequate to situation. The power of material or occasion intimidates language as the authority of perfect attitude and the power of a perfect speaker intimidates our speaking. But material stimulates language as well, calls it forth, and the image of a totally adequate language affirms the possibilities and powers of human speech. The language of a narrative, then, lies between the silence of material and the silence of attitude in two senses: Without language material and attitude are not actualized, and always do the two defy perfect and total actualization. The nature of language in narrative is this: It is the only reality, yet it derives from and sacrifices itself to the possibilities of material and attitude.[22]

It may, in closing, be appropriate to clarify these matters further by responding to a specific formulation of them by a theological aesthetician, Fr. William Lynch.[23] Lynch construes what I am here calling material and attitude as particulars and truth. By opposing the manipulation of particulars or material in the name of truth or attitude, such as, for example, using particulars as reflections of the self or expressing disgust with particulars through flight to some spiritual realm, Lynch advocates what he calls the analogical mind, namely, the mind that perceives and discloses the actual coincidence of details and design, particulars and their truth. This analogical mind opposes what Lynch takes to be distortions, namely, the univocal mind, which subjects material to ideas, and the equivocal mind, which sacrifices judgment and attitude before the force of the multiplicity and confusion of facts. But Lynch's theological undergirding to his aesthetic theory—in which world equals creation, human equals Christian, and time equals Christ's redemptive life—cuts off aesthetic possibilities. As I indicated, language need not always create a coincidence between material and attitude. Language can favor material, the silence prior to word; it can move in favor of attitude, the silence of adequate word; and it can call attention to the act itself, the use of language. Lynch's rejection of literature that appears to suffer from the angelism of fascination for perfect attitude or his rejection of a literature reduced to or anesthetized by the sheer multiplicity and confusion of particulars and events, cuts off aesthetic and spiritual possibilities. Perhaps a balance between the three aspects of tone—material, language, and attitude—can be held out as aesthetically the most pleasing, but narratives which turn us primarily to one

22. With this formulation I view the "abolition of art" not as only a recent phenomenon, but as a tendency in the aesthetic use of language generally. See Susan Sontag, "The Aesthetics of Silence" in her *Styles of Radical Will* (New York: Dell Publishing Co., 1969), especially p. 5. On the other hand, my comments here are not opposed to most of her observations in this essay, particularly her statement, "Silence, then, is both the precondition of speech and the result or aim of properly directed speech" (p. 23).
23. William F. Lynch, *Christ and Apollo: The Dimensions of the Literary Imagination* (New York: New American Library, 1963).

of the three should not be dismissed as aesthetically or religiously heretical.

In this chapter, then, we have looked at a fourth answer to the question, Why do narratives carry or generate religious or religiously suggestive meanings? They do because tone, one of the elements of narrative, is an imitation of the creative moment when material, language, and attitude are made one, a moment that has important associations with relation and wholeness, with, consequently, affirmation and belief. When reflected upon, then, tone naturally takes to itself enrichments and complications from that moment of religious life and thought having to do with religious experience, orientation, and response.

Conclusion

I

In this conclusion I intend to address the characteristics of religion more directly so that it can be made clearer what it is in religious life and thought to which the elements of narrative stand in a roughly parallel relation. Before doing that, something should be said about the general problem of defining the term "religion" in the atmosphere of the modern university. What I have particularly in mind is that the method of defining "religion" depends very much on the atmosphere in which it is defined. Also, I think that attitudes toward the term and toward the study of that which it can be thought to refer have changed.

Rather recently, religion and the study of it have moved from an earlier acceptance through a period of rejection and suspicion. The earlier acceptance was based largely on reverence for religion or for those who were spokesmen for it or who studied it, even though questions concerning the nature of religion and the validity of studying religion were also very much a part of the atmosphere. Under the increasing pressure of suspicion and even hostility toward the study of religion, changes in that study took place. For one thing, departments of religion became confessionally pluralistic, taking into themselves the societal conditions which, to a degree, caused some of the suspicion and hostility. More importantly, the study of religion was put on the defensive, and departments of religion defined their activity somewhat negatively, that is, as acting on a responsibility for doing kinds of things not done in other departments. Because of an epistemology which tended to exclude religion from serious consideration, less "religious" but still elusive matters, such as value questions, became difficult for the university to deal with.

Indeed, at some points, it began to appear that to study religion was to do kinds of things which could or would not be done in the rest of the university, and departments came to be marked to some degree by indeterminateness and even defiance. A final consequence of this pressure of suspicion or hostility was the uneasiness which scholars of religion felt among themselves toward the term "religion," their tendency to absorb the suspicion of those around them and to undercut, therefore, the term of their identity. They began to dissolve the study of religion in some larger concern, such as the way people cope with the disvalues of anxiety, guilt, or dread, the ways in which people orient themselves spatially and temporally, or the experience of and quest for meaning or value. Also, the study of literature in departments of religion may perhaps be attributed, at least in part, to an interest in some aspect of human life that was taken to be more universal and more generally accepted than religion, to an interest in undercutting the religious with the aesthetic, a move often fortified with some Arnoldian concept of culture or some Tillichian concept of ultimate concern.

We are now, however, in a period of growing acceptance toward religion and the study of it. Granted increasingly, it seems, is the possibility that there is such a thing as a religious person, act, or thing, that if there are such they should be studied in their religiousness, and that this religiousness can be studied. Those granting this new acceptance may not know how one goes about determining what is religious and how it ought to be studied or why that study is worthwhile, but they accept the possibility that work along these lines could and should be done.

The process of identifying and approaching religion in a climate of acceptance[1] is different in some respects from attempting such things in a period of systematic doubt and basic suspicion. Under the pressure of systematic doubt and under a method of reducing matters to their simplest components, "religion" would have to be defined as a term referring to something which could be demonstrated as not reducible to sociological, say, or psychological components. In a situation of acceptance, at least hypothetical assent could be expected to the proposal, Let us treat

---

1. Wayne C. Booth, *Modern Dogma and the Rhetoric of Assent* (Chicago: University of Chicago Press, 1974).

religious people as though they were religious. In a situation of assent there can be assumed an agreement that the word "religion" or "religious" may refer to something, that what it refers to can be appropriately studied, and that doing so is worthwhile.

What is necessary in that situation is to define the term by listing religion-making characteristics.[2] When these are agreed upon, one can call "religious" whatever possesses or can be imagined to possess those characteristics. That which possesses fewer than all of them or possesses them incompletely could be called less than religious, religiously suggestive, or religious-like. It should be remembered, however, that such characteristics stand at some distance from religion itself; that is, they are aids for the outsider. A religious person would not understand himself in the terms about to be suggested; the characteristics are a step away from a person and his religion. For one thing, such characteristics are general, and people and their religions are not. More importantly, general characteristics of this kind deny something of great importance to a particular religion, namely, its claim to ultimacy. We are always dealing with religion, then, as though it were something other or less than what those whose it is take it to be.

II

The first characteristic of a religious person is that he is primarily oriented toward what he cannot understand or control, and he is primarily oriented to it because he considers it primary in all important ways: being, power, and worth. There is, it seems to me, no way out of this tautology and no need to see it as carrying certain kinds of philosophical assertions first of all. If we are to allow that a religious person is worth taking seriously in ways different from other kinds of people, we have to allow that this should not be reduced to something else or established by or dependent upon something else. Of course, this orientation may be thought of as containing other components— projections, for example, arising out of a desire for a perfect father figure or for a return to the unity and stillness of the womb, or casual metaphysical and axiological assertions. But we are asked not to consider such components as exhaustive of, or

2. See William P. Alston, *Religious Belief and Philosophical Thought* (New York: Harcourt, Brace & World, 1963), p. 5.

primary to, the characteristic. And the force of this first characteristic must be kept in mind: What a person cannot understand or control is taken by him to be more important, more valuable, more potent, and more enduring than what he can understand or control. Also, that to which he is oriented is not beyond understanding and control in the sense that a problem to which we do not yet have an answer is still beyond us. Rather, the religious person is oriented to what he recognizes is *always* beyond understanding and control.

The second religion-making characteristic—and it should be repeated that these three characteristics cannot be taken in isolation from one another but constitute, instead, a whole—is that a religious person is one for whom this which is always beyond his understanding and control is also in some way in the person's world, or is somehow made available, or to some degree accessible. This is that characteristic of religion which accounts for forms, models, figures or intermediaries, on the one hand, or rituals on the other. That is, this which is beyond understanding and control has to do with the religious person or he has to do with it; separation or alienation from it is a temporary, or secondary, or derived state. A religious person has some kind or degree of relationship with what he cannot understand or control, and this relation is made possible for him or expressed to him through some form: figures and rituals.

The third religion-making characteristic is that the relation of a religious person to what he cannot understand or control through the forms of the religion has an effect on the person, changes him in a some radical way, gives him some unique benefit, or imposes some special obligation. That is, the religious person accounts in some way for what he is, possesses, or does by referring to what he cannot understand or control, as that has been related to him in a form.

I do not intend these characteristics to seem eccentric but rather to at least approximate the kind of definition of "religion" or "religious" a reader could be expected to accept as workable. I trust, in other words, that they do not damage the possibility of acceptance by making strange or exaggerated demands on a reader. Furthermore, if we can imagine him as doing so, a religious person encountering these characteristics would not be offended when once it was pointed out that these characteristics always stand at a distance from what any actual religious person is or understands himself to be. Students of religion, particularly of Eastern religions, may find the characteristics provincial, culture-bound, and Western. Of course, the very act in which we are engaged is culture-bound and Western, but the characteristics themselves do not strike me as necessarily descriptive of Western religions only. Rather, they are intended as descriptive of any religious person to the degree that any culture-bound categories can be descriptive of a phenomenon outside that culture. Furthermore, I would want to urge that in relation to any particular religion or religious person the student should be eager to modify his list of characteristics. Finally, and most importantly, I would expect that, as descriptive of any particular religion at some moment or of any particular religious person, these characteristics may not have equal importance, that a wide range in emphasis may be expected. So, for example, it would not be surprising to find that the first characteristic is less important for Buddhism than it is for Islam. In fact, such a variation in emphasis can even be seen in our own religious tradition; Protestantism tends to emphasize the first, Catholicism the second, and Judaism the third of these characteristics, although no such general statement can be used to apply to every person or to every moment in these three traditions. Allowing for this variation, the presence of other characteristics in particular religions, and the distance of characteristics of this kind from any actual religion or religious person, I would propose them as heuristically useful.

At the end of each of the chapters in this study, I included a section in which I referred to the kinds of religious meanings that the elements of narrative could most naturally be thought of as attracting to themselves when once they were reflected upon. What I was there suggesting can now be summarized more explicitly.

Reflection on atmosphere leads to a consideration of otherness, of those conditions of life which the characters or narrator cannot change. Reflection on otherness leads to contemplation of what cannot be controlled or, even, understood. The aspects of religious life and thought which such reflection would naturally lead to, then, are those related to the first of the religion-making characteristics. Otherness and what cannot be understood or controlled are, as we suggested, middle terms between the element of atmosphere and the first religion-making characteristic. This is not a way of saying that what atmosphere is to fiction, God is, say, to a Christian; it suggests, merely, a parallel relation, particularly one which accounts for the way in which reflection on atmosphere can easily lead to discussions or images of the transcendent.

Reflection on characters, as we suggested, can naturally lead to consideration of human possibilities, and characters are or can be paradigms of such possibilities. As paradigms they can easily be construed, by what was called "ascending symbolism," as reminiscent of religiously authoritative figures—Prometheus, Buddha, or Jesus. Reflection on the status of characters as paradigms of human possibilities, then, takes naturally to itself aspects of the second religion-making characteristic, namely, those forms of religious life which are figures, models, mediators, or deliverers. Again, by talking both of the relation of character as paradigm and of the religious forms of religious life which are figures, models, mediators, or deliverers we are in some middle ground between what character always is for fiction and what an authoritative figure is for a religious community, but we indicate thereby what kind of religious meanings can easily begin to be suggested when character is reflected upon.

The third element of narrative we treated, plot, can, as we saw, be suggestive of basic social, psychic, or natural processes, and reflection on plot can naturally lead not only to that association, but also to religiously suggestive indications of ritual, since rituals, with whatever more they are in a religion—and they are much more!—do take into themselves kinds of time which suggest social, psychic, and natural processes. For this reason, it can be said that when the status and nature of plot are complicated and enriched, images can easily and naturally be drawn from the second religion-making characteristic, too, namely, those religious forms which are rituals.

Finally, the element of tone, as we saw, is an image of wholeness and relation within the creative act, particularly a relation of material, attitude, and language to one another and, also, the sense of the wholeness of atmosphere, character, and plot. Tone naturally has a relation, then, to such aspects of human experience as testimony, affirmation, and belief. When these are enriched or complicated with religiously suggestive associations, those associations are derived from the third of the religion-making characteristics, namely, from the effect on the devotee, his experience of receiving, believing, and responding to the power, being, or value of what cannot be understood and controlled, made available to him in religious forms, and fundamentally determining his life in the world.

The answer to the question, Why do narratives so often and so easily complicate and enrich themselves with meanings that are religiously suggestive or apparently religious?, then, is that they do because the elements of narrative stand to the characteristics of religion like two walls of a canyon stand to each other, separated but with structural matching points. It is for this reason that religious power and meaning have been so often in the past, and in the present still can be, expressed in stories, and, more to the point of this discussion, that consciousness of the elements of narrative—and we live in a period in which artists are conscious of the potential and problems in the elements of narrative—can lead to images and ideas which indicate counterparts in religious life and thought. Moreover, it is possible, given this resemblance between the particular elements and the particular characteristics, to say what kind of religious meaning a narrative will take to itself when one rather than some other of its elements is operating as its principal power and meaning source. Between narrative and religion, then, there exists an open area, so to speak, in which the two can extend themselves or across which a theorist can cast some lines. This area is indicated by a narrative when an element is reflected upon, complicated, and enriched; from the other side, this area is indicated when religious life and thought are described in terms of general characteristics such as those I have used, characteristics which at one time are both less than religious and suggestive of components of a human world. The words I have used in the titles to chapters in this study indicate possible moments of convergence within this area: otherness, paradigm, process, and belief.

What fiction has in common with religion is a fund of resources to constitute an entire world. I would call a "world" the organic relation of inclusive and potentially exhaustive elements or characteristics, such as those at which we have been looking.

As Robert Bellah puts it:

> . . . the need to integrate the whole, known and unknown, conscious and unconscious, grows stronger. Somehow or other men must have a sense of the whole. They must have something to believe in and to commit themselves to.[3]

So closely does Bellah identify the aesthetic and the religious need and capacity to provide wholes that he is willing to take the imagined wholes of literary works to constitute the major, if not exclusively viable, source of images of a world, of symbols of the whole within modern society. Although his identification of the aesthetic with the religious is helpful in underscoring the point, it should be clear by this time why I draw back from that solution to the question of the relation between the two.

III

Although fictions as imagined worlds do a unifying work which, in a pluralistic as well as an at least partially skeptical society, religious wholes cannot, I would suggest that religious wholes cannot be collapsed into their aesthetic counterparts. Consequently, it may be suitable to end this discussion by turning now to religion and to ask briefly how it would view the kind of narratives about which we have been talking. In other words, need the lines of connection be thrown only from the one side? First we should say what accounts for an anticipated uneasiness on the part of a religious person in the face of these rough correlations between narrative elements and the characteristics of his religiously structured world; we go on, after that, to indicate reasons for easing this resistance.

For example, what is the otherness of fictional atmosphere to a person for whom the transcendent has already a place of primacy in his world? Very likely it is a threat or poor substitute. Plato was engaged by this matter in the *Republic*. For him there are two worthy enterprises for poets—to praise the gods and to praise great men who help to create and maintain the state. That

3. Robert N. Bellah, "Transcendence in Contemporary Piety," in *Transcendence*, ed. Herbert Richardson and Donald Cutler (Boston: Beacon Press, 1969), p. 96.

is, poets do an acceptable work when they subject themselves to more important matters, the transcendent world and the world of everyday. But when they create alternative or possible worlds subjected neither to the ideas nor to responsible life in community, they become a threat. Sir Philip Sidney felt called upon to defend poetry against puritan forms of ideas such as these, particularly the charge that poetry had no authority. He could only defend it by construing the function of poetry as teaching and delighting, by subjecting poetry to larger truths, by understanding its symbols as "descending" (to use a term from a distinction I noted earlier on). But what happens in a situation such as our own in which otherness is projected, imaged, or hypothesized as primarily true for the work, but then secondarily and ambiguously related to extraneous understandings of the world? We have, in fact, a situation of separation between the integrity of the otherness in narrative, its autonomy or freedom from higher laws, and that in religious life to which a term like "otherness" refers. Otherness in a fiction is not the same thing as that to which the term "the transcendent" in religious life refers for a religious person. On the other hand, the two can converge as atmosphere in a fiction is reflected upon and complicated by religiously suggestive associations and as the reader, rooted in his own sense of the primacy of what cannot be understood or controlled, feels free to imagine himself into a fictional world.

Second, whatever can be said of the status of the transcendent for a religious person can, by implication, also be said of his attitude toward those religiously authoritative forms in which or through which he believes the transcendent to be connected to his world or made accessible to him. These forms will likely be taken as authoritative and complete. They will sum up all possibilities. And the religious man would expect the characters and plots of narratives to be illustrative of, or in other ways dependent upon, these forms if they are to have validity and force. Dissociated from or antagonistic to these totally adequate forms, fictional characters could easily be taken by him as creating distorted images of human life and unhealthy emotions in readers, a charge of Plato's that may have been Aristotle's intention to refute in the *Poetics*. This situation is exacerbated in the present by plots and characters which seem not only far

from religious figures and rituals but also in themselves cor-
rupting and base. Edmund Fuller, for example, asserts:

> Most of the picture of man projected in our fiction is the ob-
> vious product of despairing self-hatred, extended from the indi-
> vidual self to the whole race of men, with its accompanying
> will to degradation and humiliation. It is a clinical condition.[4]

A religious person could argue that what is needed are paradigmatic figures and plots in narrative that would deepen and
enrich the sense of human life, and theologians such as Dietrich
von Hildebrand deplore what they call "sin mysticism" in contemporary writers, a fascination with perversity.[5] However, if
authors do give us paradigms of human possibility in characters
and images of processes in plots, we can expect from them characters and plots which stand beyond or take us beyond the pale
of acceptable social behavior. Violence and sex often, for example, are not dealt with perversely, but as modes of undercutting or transcending the unnecessary limitations of a situation
or of exploring possibilities as yet unestablished. In any event,
the forms of religious life and the characters and plots of narrative move toward one another through those elaborations, transfigurations, and pseudonyms of which we spoke earlier,[6] and
fictional images of ritual correlate with the religious person's
interest in seeing instances of human possibility and meaningful time fleshed out in a contemporary experiment.

Finally, the religious element of response finds its rough correlation in the image of the creative act within the work, the
element of tone. We can easily guess that there may be some
tension in the relation of response for a religious person to what
Poirier calls the "performing self" or to what Paul Zweig sees
as the heresy of self-love in Western literature.[7] The tension is

---

4. Edmund Fuller, *Man in Modern Fiction: Some Minority Opinions on
Contemporary American Writing* (New York: Random House, 1949), p. 4.
5. Dietrich von Hildebrand, *True Morality and Its Counterfeits* (New
York: David McKay Co., 1950), p. 44.
6. See, e.g., Edwin Moseley, *Pseudonyms of Christ in the Modern
Novel: Motifs and Methods* (Pittsburgh: University of Pittsburgh Press,
1961); Theodore Ziolkowski, *Fictional Transfigurations of Jesus* (Princeton: Princeton University Press, 1972); and Robert McAfee Brown,
Pseudonyms of God (Philadelphia: Westminster Press, 1972).
7. Paul Zweig, *The Heresy of Self-Love: A Study of Subversive Indi-
vidualism* (New York: Harper & Row, 1968).

aggravated by what is commonly referred to as the solipsism, the intense subjectivity of recent literature.[8] In the religious world the self is derived, gifted, even created; in the modern fictional world it is self-made and determinative. Yet the two worlds move toward one another as it is recognized that the occasion and ability to use language in a literary work is derived at least to some degree from indebtedness to material and to the sense of some responsibility to an image or possibility of perfect judgment, and when it is recognized by a religious man that his response to the transcendent within religious forms must also be his own.

In other words, while I consider it mistaken to call the imagined world of a narrative religious, and while I am aware of points of tension between the narrative whole and that world structured by the characteristics of religion, narratives do help to clarify and give, so to speak, concrete instances of those major matters of which a religious man's life are constituted. Also, while it has not been the purpose of this discussion to elaborate on it, it could be said that religion needs narratives to grant to it such instances. There are also, then, reasons why religious people in the past and, perhaps, in the present, create, read, and value narrative. In the introduction, I suggested that, in general, people write or read narratives because those acts have a striking resemblance to religious acts, attitudes, and ideas. However, we have turned our attention in this discussion to texts, to narratives themselves, in order to ask the question, Why do they so often carry religious or religiously suggestive meanings? The answer we have given is this, Although they stand as well at some distance from one another, the elements of narrative are correlatives of the characteristics of religion.

---

8. See, e.g., some studies of the religious implications of this individuality: Stanley R. Hopper, "The Problem of Moral Isolation in Contemporary Literature," in *Spiritual Problems in Contemporary Literature*, ed. Stanley R. Hopper (New York: Harper and Brothers, 1952), pp. 153–173; Nathan A. Scott, "Society and the Self in Recent American Literature" in his *The Broken Center: Studies in the Theological Horizon of Modern Literature* (New Haven: Yale University Press, 1966); and Wesley A. Kort, "Recent Fiction and Its Religious Implications," *Comparative Literature Studies* (1966): particularly pp. 226–29.

Index

116